THE CADET;

A POEM,

In Six Parts:

CONTAINING

REMARKS ON BRITISH INDIA.

TO WHICH IS ADDED,

EGBERT AND AMELIA;

In Four Parts:

WITH

OTHER POEMS.

BY

A LATE RESIDENT IN THE EAST.

" . . . . . . 'Tis better to be lowly born,
" And range with humble livers in content,
" Than to be perk'd up in a glitt'ring grief,
" And wear a golden sorrow."—SHAKSPEARE.

IN TWO VOLUMES.

VOL. I.

LONDON:

PRINTED FOR ROBERT JENNINGS, 2, POULTRY,

BY J. MOYES, GREVILLE STREET.

1814.

PREFACE

THE FIRST VOLUME.

———————

UNPATRONISED and unknown, the Author of the following sheets sends his little book into the world. It may possibly drop from the press, with many others, which Fame shall reject as unworthy; and may be doomed, with them, to sail down the daily current of chance, until, pelted at by the swarms from the critic hive, it may miss the haven of popularity; and overwhelmed, at

length, by the blustering squalls of splenetic
censure, sink never again to rise. However, in
the candour of the judicious shall I place my
trust; and the result may show to me, that being
unknown is not an infallible passport to disappointment, or always a just reason for being
mocked at.

Be it told to his readers, that the Author of
these little volumes is a very young man; and,
when the poems contained in them were written,
was still a minor. If this in nothing concern the
public, it nevertheless materially concerns himself to tell it; for, if any thing be approved of
in these adolescent labours, it may not unna-
turally be inferred, that the strength of manhood
might hereafter produce something of more sterling worth: and the critics, too, may possibly
bestow somewhat of encomium on the following writings, as the effusions of youth; when
they might probably be inclined to attack them

with severity, as the studied efforts of maturer age.

I confess myself to suspect, that, if I have scattered any flowers among the following numerous leaves, they are so choked by weeds as to be almost hidden: still, if any thing like blossom can be selected from the mass of rude and uncultivated growth which may surround them, I am led to hope that the learned critic will hold it up to a favourable light, where all who wish to gaze may see it to advantage; and, transplanted into his elegant literary conservatory, it will no doubt improve it's growth, and enhance it's claim to public approbation, by a change of soil.

The longest of the poems here offered to general notice, is " THE CADET." The tale in blank verse was at first intended to be sent alone into the world, as the Preface to it evinces: however, after-thoughts induced the Author to

join them, and thus are they given together.
The subjects which compose the first poem
may prove in some degree offensive to such
as are partial to India; as therein that country
is painted in no very flattering colours: however,
the Author would rather run the hazard of
offending them, than blot from his pages one
of the many severe truths which they may
contain.

, He who gave to form the present volumes,
left England as a Cadet somewhat more than
four years ago; chiefly induced by the dear idea
of meeting a father, whom, since the earliest
period of infancy, he had but once seen:—
shortly after his arrival he heard of his death:—
he discovered, much to his disappointment, nothing on the Continent of Asia to interest him,
nothing to make him compensation for the severe
sacrifice made in leaving his friends and paternal
residence; he became unhappy; whilst his chief,

and indeed almost only, pleasure was derived from the ever gratifying recreation of reading, and committing to paper at times the wild conceits of his fancy. Some few observations on India he drew up into a poetic form, and these are now offered to the public under the title of " THE CADET." The attempt is possibly a very humble one; nevertheless, as a juvenile production, it may bear some claim to attention; and particularly when it is considered, that the whole was composed where the Author had no access to books, beyond the few which he was enabled to carry about with him; and those were indeed but few.

I can, or at least I fancy I can, foresee where some of the sharper points of criticism will be directed: I shall silently await the punishment; and, without murmuring, bear the wound that may be inflicted.

My greatest appreheniosn is, lest the frowns of
the fair be excited by what appears against them
in the following pages : but let it be remembered
that it is the females of British India alone who
are glanced at; and, indeed, only some of them.—
I know so many estimable women, that I never
can think otherwise than honourably and ten-
derly of the sex, and stand forth in their favour
as a true believer, that, whilst follies are im-
puted to them without number, they are but
follies, against which the ruder creature man
frequently opposes *crimes*. Be here to them my
reparation for any offence they may have taken
against me, that I consider the world to be
indebted to them for it's fairest ornament. Man
is the sublimer creature certainly; woman the
more beautiful. She is the strong attractive
power which binds man to discretion; and
often curbs the rein of imprudence, when

he is hurrying onward to the hidden toil of destruction.

In the description of the *Establishment*, truth has been rigidly adhered to, as well as in every other part of the poem, where speculative matter does not interfere.

The general picture of India is drawn, I must grant, by no means from a favourable impression; but it was taken just as it appeared presented to my observation.

The Cadet leaves this country full of vague expectations, occasioned by specious stories which he constantly hears of the luxurious pleasures of an Oriental clime. He leaves his home, and every thing that has fixed his heart's attachment, and on arriving at the region which fancy, when at a distance from it, had painted in such expressive colours, reality bursts the airy bubble, and leaves him to his disappointment. He generally—too young, probably, to be under his own guidance—commences a career of voluptuous pleasure and blind dissipation; he meets with numbers to encourage him; and not uncommonly, in the very May-day of existence, falls a victim to the extravagant folly of excess.

Many, it has been said, make large fortunes in India, return to this country, and enjoy them. True it is, indeed, that some do; but they are as the eyes of the head in comparison to the hairs, two only to multitudes. Those few who do return are always heard of; whilst the thousands that fail in the desired acquisition of riches, and become martyrs either to the virulence of the climate, or to the prevailing but baneful effects of habitual dissipation, fall into the gulf of oblivion silently, and unheard of, but by the few.

I shall now close this Preface by deprecating

unnecessary critical severity, and venturing a
hope, that, where the Critic finds himself ne-
cessitated to withhold commendation, that he
will, at least, bestow censure with manly
candour.

CONTENTS

OF

THE FIRST VOLUME.

THE CADET.

Part the First.

" Væ misero mihi, quanta de spe decidi !"—TERENCE.

DELUDED Youth! as Rumour swells the gale,
And Fancy spreads her visionary sail, —
When joys uncurb'd thy buoyant mind beguile,
And infant Pleasure yields her meetest smile;
Thine artless ear imbibes the frequent lie,
That Earth's best blessings show'r from India's sky;
That Nature sheds profusion o'er the soil,
Nor asks the ruder drudgery of toil;
That Flora empties her abundant vase,
And Eden's treasures glad the swarthy race.

Thou hear'st that wealth by little heed is gain'd,
And life at no important cost maintain'd;
That ev'ry bliss ambitious man can know,
Is here secur'd, nor ever dash'd with wo. —
Accurs'd Deceit! What cares have birth from thee!
How oft the source of stinging Misery!
Unweening boy! 'tis Falsehood's voice you hear,
Prompt to deceive — to drain Affliction's tear:
Avoid the fiend, nor trust his courtly smiles;
For he, when least suspected, most beguiles.
But 'tis too late, the resolution's ta'en,
Nor babbling Rumour wafts his lies in vain.

Warm'd at his specious tale, thy bosom glows
To view that plenty which this clime bestows:
Now, crude of judgment, all thy soul on fire,
To realize some vague, unknown desire,
Rous'd inclination, slackens Prudence' rein,
And from the sober durance of the brain
Discretion flees; whilst unrestricted will
Escapes restraint, nor heeds the chance of ill:
Golconda's treasures dance before thine eyes,
And thy warm'd mind forms castles in the skies:
But soon Experience beats those fabrics down,
Rends Fancy's veil, and shows Truth's awful frown.

Thy skiff, just launch'd into the sea of life,
And all thy wishes, with thy weal at strife;
Thy mind on wildest expectations bent,
Whilst ev'ry hope runs counter to content;
Thou hear'st, weak boy, false Rumour's luring voice,
And undigested whim directs thy choice:
Imagination, deck'd in pageant robe,
Paints the false splendours of a torrid globe;
Draws on the easy tablets of the mind
A dazzling picture, scarce of earthly kind:
Like fabl'd Midas, long renown'd of old,
All that it rests upon, converts to gold;
Buoys up thy heart, to mark what Rumour tells,
And casts profuse Infatuation's spells—
Conception strengthens at an empty theme,
As untaught children credit what they dream.

Now, all too thoughtless to detect the cheat,
Thou hear'st the baleful accents of Deceit;
And, 'guil'd by common Fame, ideas vain
Prompt the mad wish to cross the Indian main:
Reflection's hush'd, Consideration flies,
And rash Imprudence either's place supplies;
Thou rushest eager to the goal of wo,
And view'st, ere long, Contentment's overthrow:

Thy heart that late on hope expanding swell'd,
Where Fancy beam'd, too radiant to be quell'd,
Now droops·o'erburthen'd, impotent to bear
The load that Disappointment places there.
Thus the gay fly upon the solar beam,
Oft flits fantastic o'er the ripling stream,
,Till, heedless grown, the mirror'd wave he tries,
Flutters awhile his little wings, and dies.

Before thine eyes those mighty realms survey,
Where Sol confirms a more resplendent day ;
Secure in thought, of ev'ry nobler joy
That man can taste, unmingled with alloy ;
Of ample competence, luxurious ease,
All that the most fastidious mind may please :
Thy quick imagination instant draws
Pictures of bliss beyond kind Nature's laws :
But, when thy feet impress th' ungenial shore,
Those air-rear'd structures fall, to rise no more !
When once the rashly fatal die is thrown,
Vain is repentance, vain Affliction's moan. —
When landed once on Ind's unsocial waste,
Should thy late sprightly heart admit distaste —
Should Disappointment give thee cause to mourn,
Sorrow thou must, for thou can'st not return :

No wealth* to aid thee, here must thou remain,
And sighs are heav'd, and tears are shed in vain.

Why did'st thou listen to the treach'rous tales,
That wealth is blown on Oriental gales;
That spicy breezes waft perfumes around,
And Earth's best produce loads the fruitful ground;
That here man wears the vestments of Content,
Whilst Peace supports her firm establishment;
That Plenty e'er unloads her teeming horn,
And often squanders from Profusion's urn?
Did'st thou conceive, as fabulists have told,
That Eastern rocks are form'd of massy gold?
That copious wealth descends with vernal show'rs,
And lolling Lux'ry lightens lagging hours?
That gems refulgent sparkle o'er the sands†,
Whilst vast abundance freights the various lands.

* It is a fact but too melancholy, that many young men,
whose inclinations on arriving in India would lead them to
return, are compelled, from a want of money to pay their
passage home, to remain in a country, probably neither congenial to the constitution of their minds nor bodies; and, in consequence, spend a life of listless apathy, or of uncontrolled
dissipation.

† Although the general idea of India may not be precisely
such as the above insinuates; yet certain it is, that there

Deluded stripling ! short thy date of bliss !
Experience quickly proves you thought amiss :
When once you land beneath an orient sky,
Your visions cease, your dear delusions die ;
Chill Disappointment rears his frowning head,
And sternly shows that all your hopes are fled !
Fancy no longer works ; the downcast eye
Beholds a sadly drear reality ;
Harsh Discontent assails the pensive breast,
And robs it frequent of it's dearest rest.

Flow fast my tears ! let Anguish have it's way,
Since goading Grief will make the heart her prey.
Why did I madly leave the home I lov'd,
To seek a realm where Care's so frequent prov'd ?
Well may I mourn the folly of my choice,
And curse the hour I dwelt on Falsehood's voice.
Did not Deception lull the youthful mind,
How few would leave their parent homes behind !
Leave that fond Isle, by hope entic'd alone,
Where ev'ry joy of social bliss is known ;
Where Freedom fosters her illustrious sons,
Whilst her pure current unimpeded runs ?

prevails an opinion of fortunes being so rapidly made in
this country, that any one who can get out here is provided
for.—It often proves a calamitous delusion.

Where lust of fame, and laudable desire,
Fan in the patriot breast it's noblest fire;
Strike from the flint of apathy a spark,
That warms the soul, and lights where it is dark ;
Dispels the clogging frost of unconcern,
And gives the brightest torch of zeal to burn ;
Where the free people love their King and Laws,
Nor pause at peril in their Country's cause ;
Where Valour's thron'd pre-eminently high,
And firmly clasps the zone of Liberty —
Oh! may this feeble effort be forgiv'n!
To sing her praises needs a Muse from Heav'n.

Could the young adult, ere he quits his home,
Gaze on those realms o'er which he sighs to roam,
His wishes would expire ; his eager eyes
Droop into dull and stupified surprise:
No cheering ray of pleasure would there beam,
If dull reality dispell'd the dream ;
For 'tis no better what the mind conceives,
By fancy pregnant, when it thus believes,
That God in India most delights to bless,
And here grants most abundant happiness.
Could he who pants a torrid soil to roam,
See it in contrast with his dearer home,

The eager wish, which fill'd his mind before,
Would die away, and harrass it no more.

Here are we told that Summer ever reigns,
And Spring perpetual smiles o'er Indian plains;
That wheresoe'er the wand'ring feet may tread,
Beneath they find the richest verdure spread;
That from the shrubs the choicest sweets exhale,
And with ambrosial fragrance load the gale;
That bland Pomona decorates the earth,
And spreads the carpet wove at Nature's birth*;
That fruits and blossoms gild the circling year,
Whilst songs of transport glad the list'ning ear;
That feather'd warblers give their choice delight,
Whilst Bulbul †, whistling to the ear of Night,
Sheds o'er the wounded heart a soothing balm,
And turns the soul's tornado into calm.

How false the tale! the spacious land adust,
Unnourish'd, mourns at Nature's scanty trust;
Each wither'd shrub reclines it's sun-burnt head,
And the pain'd eye marks vegetation dead;

* Some parts of India have been compared to the Garden of Eden.
† A species of nightingale.

Gapes the parch'd earth, the wither'd herbage dies,
And the lean cattle mourn their lost supplies ;
Stray o'er the steril ground, with eager gaze,
Seeking some friendly spot where they may graze :
Yet nought is found, tho' pass'd be many a glade,
But here and there a solitary blade *.
The screaming paroquet distends his throat,
Oft answer'd by the raven's croaking note ;
The early crow, ere morning streaks the East,
Upon the house-top takes his matin rest ;
And hoarsely cawing, limits Slumber's reign,
Nor, 'till the sun rides lofty, seeks the plain.—
'Twere bold, perhaps presumptuous, to avow
The nightingale of India is — the crow †.

It must be own'd the Epicure may find,
In ev'ry season, fruits of various kind ;
The guava, melon, plantain, and the pine,
With all the gen'rous produce of the vine ;

* This, it must be confessed, does not at all tally with the
general descriptions given of India : however, I was for some
months in one of the most fertile provinces of Hindostan, and
could perceive scarcely any thing of vegetation, but during the
rains.

† Crows are plentiful in India, even to a nuisance.

Still no productions of an orient field,
A pleasing flavour to the palate yield;
Vapid and flat the sick'ning moisture cloys,
Weighs on the stomach, and the taste destroys:
Chokes oft the grosser avenue of sense,
And adds another mite to Indolence *.

Be 't e'en admitted that Vertumnus pours
O'er Indian fields the choicest of his stores;
Can that compensate for those pungent woes,
Those mighty ills, which Ind so frequent knows?
Evils sometimes so horribly severe,
As from the dryest eye would force the tear.

Oft griping Famine, with her craving band,
Stalks vengeful forth, and wastes the thirsting land;
Heart-rending horrors follow in her train,
And frighted Nature deprecates in vain:
Death smiles triumphant, marks the mournful wo,
Bares his gaunt arm, and strikes the forceful blow:

---

* The fruits in this country are mostly flat to the taste;
the grape is almost the sole exception : even the boasted pine-
apple is frequently little better than a turnip. The fruits here,
which are generally eaten in abundance, cloy the stomach, and
render the body listless; the couch is then resorted to : — first
amongst Indian luxuries.

Whole nations feel the shock, and trembling cow'r
Beneath the tyrant's devastating pow'r:
Thousands on thousands, from life's summit hurl'd,
Gasp out their last, and seek a holier world!
Wo, grief, want, sorrow, beggary arise,
And swell their mingled clamours to the skies:
Earth gashly groans beneath the load of Death,
And blasts the air with foul Contagion's breath.

Are such the blessings Indian climes afford?
Is this where Plenty opes her secret hoard?
Where bright Creation wears Spring's vernal vest,
And favour'd man can never but be blest?
'Tis falsehood all, for ev'ry day we see
That here's the dark domain of Misery.
Here ever rests, too potent not to please,
The baleful agent of accurs'd Disease,
Injurious Luxury, of doubtful mien,
That smoothly smiles, but stabs behind the scene.

What are the luxuries they boast them here?
The lolling couch, the joys of bottled beer:
On garnish'd sofas squeamish Misses lie,
Array'd in white, transparent drapery:
Here,—finish'd Breakfast's well display'd parade,—
They taste the sweets of beer and lemonade:

Perspiring, sleep the hasty morn away,
And scarce with noon commence the lagging day :
Now smoking meats the nasal sense regale,
And round is gayly quaff'd the sparkling ale :
In mix'd confusion men and maidens swill,
And *pious* matrons take alike their fill :
The other sex to diff'rent joys give place—
The dissipated pleasures of the chase :
Sleep half their lives, or dally with a punk,
And crown the ill spent day by getting drunk *.
Tho' here they boast them of a vernal clime,
Where scorching Summer's ever in it's prime :
What the advantage, what the blessings giv'n,
By the sublime benevolence of Heav'n ?
Rain † seldom falls to glad the rigid soil,
And yield the lab'rer recompense for toil :

* Beer is the beverage most generally preferred, I imagine,
by Europeans in India. I have not unfrequently seen ladies
drink each a large glass at a draught. The chief luxury is
lolling on a couch : eating, sleeping, driving, dress, and scandal,
follow in succession. The men hunt. The chase is called a dissipated pleasure ; because, when it is over, the sportsmen enjoy
the Indian luxury of drinking. I write as I beheld.

† The rainy season commonly lasts three months ; during
which the storms are sometimes so violent, and the rain so
excessive, as to do serious injury to the rising crops. Some

But yet sometimes the sudden deluge show'rs,
The pride of infaut harvest overpow'rs;
Destroys the bed where lies the swelling seed,
And mingles it promiscuous with the weed.

When the moist season's o'er, and brief its stay,
Again destructive shines the orb of day;
Th' unfriendly Sun his burning pow'r essays,
And every herb lies sapless 'neath his rays;
No verdant pasture gratifies the sight,
Or yields the heart that sedative delight,
Which a fine prospect never fails to lend,
When varied lands in pleasing union blend;
No daisies pied, no violets appear,
To mark the changing seasons of the year;
The glaring prospect hurts th' exploring eye,
Without one single charm to gratify.
Spring quits the region, Summer in disguise,
(Or Summer's shadow,) greets alone the eyes.

That gen'rous land, which, in eventful hour,
You left, misjudging youth, to pace no more,

seasons the rains have been known to continue no longer than
a few days; which invariably produces the most afflicting con-
sequences, for famine must ensue.

Boasts—such as stranger wilds can ne'er impart—
The strongest magnet that attracts the heart:
And what that is, let those who seek to find,
Search some far realm where man's of baser mind;
Then shall the bosom's whispers shortly tell,
The magnet's Home,—but burst the pleasing spell;—
Display the more substantial charms of home,
And prove him least content who loves to roam.
As to the North inclines the trembling steel,
E'en thus the heart, not impotent to feel,
Tends eager to the land that gave it birth,
And deems that spot the choicest upon earth.
'Tis there, when tracing out the fav'rite way,
Where active Boyhood stroll'd in sportive play,
That pliant Mem'ry conjures up to view
All that the infant mind of pleasure knew,
Tracks out the map of life, and pleas'd surveys,
The various freaks of youth's progressive days.

Imprudent fool! that Isle which you so late
Incautious left, to tempt a doubtful fate,
Boasts genuine joys, as ne'er were known to rise
Beneath the scorching glow of Eastern skies.
There, cheer'd by friends, by relatives caress'd,
With all the sweets of kindred comfort bless'd;

Nor from Society's delights debarr'd, .
Should chance Misfortune press a little hard :
Notic'd by all, who, spurning sordid aim,
Take not from merit it's deserving claim ;
There WEALTH alone no certain passport is
To *ev'ry* heart— *here gold's the spring of bliss;*
It draws love's ogle from the female eye,
And those are scorn'd who can't afford—to buy:
To the best bidder is the virgin sold,
And becomes wedded to some dotard's gold;
Drives her barouche, forgets from what she sprung,
A recent mushroom from a bed of dung—
From Britain yearly hundreds sail to try
Their luck in Asia's kinder lottery*.

Climate ungenial! Why, unartful youth,
Did you not listen to the voice of Truth ?
Why suffer Falsehood's smile to tempt you wrong,
Nor doubt the wily accents of her tongue ?

* There is nothing of exaggeration here. That many young
women go out to India on mere speculation, may defy contra-
diction: and those who do, always look out for wealthy
partners. The society of young men, however good their connexions, if unfortunately of rather inferior rank, (more particularly in the military service,) is spurned at; and by those
very women who held a rank far below mediocrity in England.

Oh! could I fix my choice ill-judg'd, again!—
The die is cast, and ev'ry wish is vain.
You, who by Hope's delusive finger led,
Now seek the land where nursling cares are fed,
Take heed! When once you tread the gloomy shore,
'Tis chance if comfort ever greet you more.

Shall e'er parental kindness meet you here,
And o'er your sorrows drop the suasive tear?
Shall Friendship ever ope his gen'rous palm,
To chase Distress, your anguish to becalm?
Shalt thou enjoy a brother's fond embrace,
Or print the kiss upon a sister's face?
And, in their lov'd society elate,
Smile on the kind vicissitudes of fate?
Here, 'mongst the shreds of beauty shalt thou find,
One who with thee shall bear congenial mind;
And by that witchery we can't express,
Cast o'er the heart love's fascinating dress?
No, here, alas! 'tis seldom thine to share
Other than sad variety of care;
For each firm link that forms the kindred tie,
Soon bursts, and strikes out Consanguinity;
Absence quick cankers that tenacious chain,
Which, sever'd once, shall ne'er unite again:

Those late endear'd too soon forget to feel,
And all their hopes revolve with Fortune's wheel.

Truth but too mournful ! He who seeks to range
O'er torrid lands, where all's severely strange,
Gull'd by false hopes, and expectations vain,
For few short pleasures meets an age of pain ;
Nor, 'till too late to remedy the wo,
Does he perceive what he must undergo ;
He's entic'd onward by imagin'd joy,
As a young babe by promise of a toy.

What are the genuine comforts India brings ?
Brutes it begets, and *reptiles arm'd with* STINGS.
Society's best pleasures all are dead,
And hamper'd etiquette prevails instead :
The Col'nel's wife demands the highest place,
And those less great must bear unjust disgrace.
Frequent you'll hear the Major's lady cry,
" Pray who taught you to hold your head so high ?
" A Captain's wife to give herself such airs !—
" I'll tell the Major, when he comes up stairs."
Then o'er the boards she takes a lengthen'd stride,
And seats her down on *Madam's* dexter side —

Here, like unkennell'd dogs, the women pother,
Growl, show their teeth, and snarl upon each other *.

The clam'rous tongue of Scandal's never still,
She slakes her thirst at Envy's bubbling rill;
Where'er she goes the hissing monster shakes
Her matted head, obscene with coiling snakes;
The squalid brood extend their gaping jaws,
And cast their venom up, against applause;
Call from her covert unrelenting Spite,
Gnash their sharp fangs at all, and strive to bite:
The reptile din incessant strikes the ear,
And gives the strictest prudence cause to fear.

How oft does silly tattling hurt repose,
And fix on Innocence unmeeted woes!
How often stamp the brand of baser fame,
Upon a noble, undeserving name!

* Thus, in this country, is the state of society: at entertainments, public and private balls, and the like, the ladies take precedence according to the rank of their respective husbands: thus the captain's lady will seat herself higher at table than the lieutenant's; the lieutenant's than the ensign's: and so through all ranks which are admitted into society. This is most particularly observed at the Indian metropolis.

What ills from trivial causes oft arise,
From what we frequent deem *unharmful* lies!
Danger e'er lurks 'neath Falsehood's kindest wing,
And when we least expect, he shows his sting.

Scandal, allied to Folly, child of Spite,
Can'st thou in softer bosoms breed delight ?
Can'st thou attaint that milder-heaving breast,
Where man on earth would seek his highest rest ?
Can'st thou o'er woman cast unseemly soil,
And turn her heart to bickering and broil ?
By sad experience *here* we're giv'n to find
It's frequent influence o'er the female mind :
How oft that baleful influence extends
To those who vaunt the dignity of friends !
Should any ask why woman is so prone,
By Scandal's shafts, to cause the griev'd to groan,
My ready answer is, 'Tis *here* alone *.

* I am not one of those who would so generally degrade the
female character, (which I esteem myself a proud admirer of,)
as to attribute to the whole sex a natural inclination to scandal.
As far as my observations on human nature have extended,
both sexes seem to me to be equally inclined to it. However,
the females in India must stand as an exception, for with them
scandal holds an exalted rank. The men are probably less

All must allow, that, put unto the test,
The noblest feelings sway the female breast:
Woman, tho' form'd in model less august
Than overbearing man may proudly boast,
Receives from Nature's hand a kinder soul;
Less stern, less rigid, fitter for controul.
How oft before her footstool humbly bows
Creation's lord, and trembling breathes his vows;
How oft she draws him to Discretion's goal,
And checks the headstrong current of his soul!
Still — What is perfect in the human plan? —
Oft hath she prov'd a bitter curse to man.

Who shall unfold what joys this country yields!
Scarce one bright tint life's gloomy prospect gilds;
No chaste enjoyments smooth the brow of Care,
No honest pleasures lull forlorn Despair;
No lofty themes of deep, instructive lore,
Regale the mind when duller labour's o'er:
No grateful pastime, save the flowing bowl,
Oft swill'd to calm the troubles of the soul —

addicted to it here, as they are not so often thrown together in
tattling parties: the chase, and other sports, keep them more
asunder. The women are always huddled together.

Here all's confusion, hurry, and dismay;
Life's track is dark, and rugged is the way.

How many hopeless maids are hither sent,
On matrimonial speculations bent!
Mere int'rest, sordid int'rest all their aim;
He most admir'd, whose wealth bears greatest claim:
Age, *juvenil'd* by gold, secures their choice,
And youth, without it, hears Scorn's ribald voice;
Receives the wanton glances of disdain, —
His sole transgression, impotence of gain. —
They set their caps at ev'ry *well-fledg'd owl*:
But, should malignant Disappointment scowl,
A last, tho' poor resource, their arts they ply,
And cast some lure at ev'ry passer by,
Entice into their toils some beardless fool,
And teach him soon to bend to female rule.
The crafty fowler thus, with hopes the same,
Neglects the small in search of nobler game:
But, should he fail in what he'd first in view,
What late he scorn'd, back turns he, to pursue;
Throws out his lure to check the smallest wing,
Content, at last, with what poor Chance may bring.
Disgust curtails the theme, nor dares to dwell
On that fair sex, so passing beautiful.

When free from follies, which sometimes infest
The nice recesses of the female breast,
The noblest feelings of the heart they claim;
It warms, it kindles, at a woman's name.

Now I'll retrace, and not without regret,
The early progress of the young CADET;
Then, thro' the after coil of fleeting years,
Follow his steps, and mark what oft appears.
Mournful my theme, and dull the task assign'd,
It casts a sadd'ning gloom upon the mind;
Whilst keen remembrance sheds her vivid rays,
And rests on blissful scenes of earlier days;
When in young Boyhood's animating prime
I gambol'd on, nor mark'd the course of time:—
But to my tale, it's melancholy strain
Noted by none, may all be rais'd in vain.

In sprightly youth's more animated hour,
When vig'rous health puts forth her brightest flow'r,
The thoughtless stripling quits that dearer land,
Where he was nourish'd by Affection's hand;
Where bliss unsullied beam'd around his head,
And kindred love his ductile heart had fed;
Bids all, rever'd on earth, a fond adieu,—
Thinking his fancied fortunes full in view—

And as the wild conceits impress his brain,
Takes the rash step, and launches on the main;
Rushes unheeding to Affliction's goal,
Where chills the finest ardour of the soul.
Too sad deceit! the vision quickly dies,
And leaves behind acute anxieties.

   The first unmeet disquietude he knows,
Where vulgar pride his taunts perpetual throws.
Within the ship that bears thee o'er the brine,
Unthinking boy, few comforts can be thine:
There may'st thou hear the voice of coarse rebuke,
From one whose soul is index'd in his look;
Who makes himself conspicuous to the crowd,
View'd like a noisy cur that barks aloud.
The rude commander of unmanly mind,
In heart a tyrant, wills not to be kind;
He knows his transient pow'r—he grasps the rod,
And makes obedience mark his haughty nod:
Coarsely disdainful, and of mind deprav'd,
Buoy'd up by arrogance, by pelf enslav'd;
From his large eyes Oppression's coward stare
Tells that ne'er Pity rais'd her tribute there.
Each undelighting hour that speeds along,
He strives to sting by some injurious wrong;

Takes base advantage—such the recreant's part—
Of ill-gain'd pow'r, to wound an honest heart,
And, when the poor disdain'd CADET goes by,
Casts down contempt's keen glances from his eye.
But the pert cock that proudest struts and cries,
When off his master's dunghil soonest flies*.

Thus, when five months have ta'en their wonted round,
Is seen the long anticipated ground,
Where the CADET, with intellectual eye,
Has frequent view'd a more benignant sky —

---

* The whole of the above is given from melancholy experience. I believe it is a practice but too common in many
India ships, to treat young men, who are on board as Cadets,
in a manner that reflects not only disgrace upon the young
men themselves, but also upon those from whom they receive
the treatment. Although they hold but an inferior rank, and
may probably be, some of them, mere boys, yet the rank they
hold is a passport even to the society of a court: and wherever
they carry with them the unexceptionable advantages of respectable connexions, a liberal education, and creditable de-
meanour, they have a right, both by Nature and the laws of
society, to the treatment of officers and gentlemen: but certain
it is, that on the passage out they do not always meet with
such. I do not rank all the captains of Indiamen as deficient
in the above respect; but, without a doubt, many may be
found who are so.

Th' expected soil, which Fancy oft has told,
A soil that teems with mines of polish'd gold —
When, all the perils of the Ocean past,
Ind's faithless shores salute his eyes at last,
How sad the disappointment! quick he finds
His hopes, long cherish'd, vanish with the winds:
Late lively mirth his throbbing breast forsakes,
And dull despondence fast possession takes.
Oft the lorn wretch, benighted on his road,
Looks round for some benevolent abode;
And hast'ning onward to some light he sees,
Finds 'twas a star, that twinkled thro' the trees.
So the CADET, in Thought's perspective, views
The pageant bliss, and instantly pursues;
He but arrives to mark the phantom fade,
And finds, too late, he strove to grasp — a shade.

END OF THE FIRST PART.

NOTE.—That this part contains much of querulous egotism, and perhaps bitter satire, I cannot attempt to deny: but where I have been severe, I sincerely believe I have been just; nor can I, from my conscience, think that the colouring of the picture is any where overcharged. The preceding was written at a time when labouring under unpleasing anxieties and galling disquietudes of mind. It is, and was, intended as nothing more than reflections on European India. If allusions to self predominate too considerably, the unhappy state of mind under which I laboured must stand my excuse with the reader. When despondency steals over us, the heart receives a melancholy satisfaction in dwelling upon it's feelings: and it must be confessed, that even in sorrow there is a kind of sedative consolation to be drawn from the very source of grief: and I derived mine frequently from dwelling, in museful mood, upon what I deemed my misery, and drawing up my complaints, observations, &c. into a poetic form.

As the tendency of my mind was every where followed throughout this writing, the digressional parts are somewhat considerable.

THE CADET.

Part the Second.

" Those who beyond sea go will surely find,
" They change their climate only, not their mind."

.... " Omnes omnia
" Bona dicere, et laudare fortunas meas."

TERENCE.

As Mem'ry wafts my thoughts to England's shore,
And pictures what these eyes may view no more;—
As from her fount the rapt'ring shadows rise,
Like distant shades that flit athwart the skies;
The sigh's exhal'd, the moist'ning tear-drops roll,
To calm the gloomy workings of the soul.
When I reflect that I have bid farewell
To that lov'd Isle where Freedom's children dwell,
Heavy prognostics shackle round my heart,
And keen Repentance wings his mightiest dart;

'Throws o'er my bosom Sorrow's sombrest stole,
And wrings, almost to agony, the soul.

Deceiv'd by common fame, more fool than wise,
I thought t' have found an earthly paradise:
India's *Elysium,* shallow Rumour cried;
But grave Experience proves the babbler lied: —
I bade my friends, my home, my all adieu,
A distant ignis fatuus to pursue.
I've left that land where centred all my joy,
Where courted peace — now lamentably coy; —
Where, from maternal throes, I sprung to light,
And helpless burst from Nature's dated night;
Where mewling Infancy engross'd awhile
A Parent's watchful care and anxious toil;
Where Reason first expanded to the view,
When baser Instinct from the brain withdrew;
Where the first mental light coruscant shin'd,
And young Idea vivify'd the mind;
Lost in the void of uncreated thought,
And to Perception's gradual climax brought.
I've left the land where peace was earliest found,
And grief was transient, impotent to wound:
Where, in more truant days, my wand'ring mind
Was of its dross corrected and refin'd;

Where the rude rust that clogg'd intelligence,
Was scatter'd by the brighter rays of sense;
Where smirking boyhood, unrestrain'd and free,
Ate the first fruits from Pleasure's purer tree.—
For, sad reverse! at this more dreary day,
As mem'ry tells what joys have pass'd away,
Stern Retrospection evidently shows,
That earliest youth the brightest season knows;
That, but too frequent, as our years increase,
We feel the more of care, the less of peace.
The laughing child, with bosom unopprest,
Innoxious pleasure sporting in his breast,
Wastes all the fleeting hours in artless play,
Without one care how speeds the time away;
Unconscious that in this world there can be,
Than parent's frown, more pungent misery.
Those days, so unillum'd, alas! are o'er,
They'll glad my blunted senses now no more:
The sombrer hues of ever-varying life
Must now be seen, exuberantly rife.
Here Retrospection can few pleasures bring,
It's ev'ry joy is furnish'd with a sting;
Contrasts awaken, galling to the heart,
Whilst Sorrow's sighs a constant gloom impart.

Mem'ry now pictures those—be check'd the tear—
Whom kindred claims have render'd ever dear:
Those, too, whom hallow'd friendship has endear'd,
And render'd worthy to be well rever'd;
Who from the soul it's first emotions claim,
And whose kind acts deserve the praise of Fame.
Those—but Prospiscience darkly shades the scene,
When I think what *may be* and what *has been.*
How chilling 'tis to dart an onward glance!
It foils the thoughts and mocks considerance:
On what *may* hap the moody mind perpends,
As dim Futurity her veil extends;
Eager to pluck the stubborn texture down,
To see if Fate assume a smile or frown:
But once prevented, Dread upholds his crest,
And heaps forebodings on the burthen'd breast.
As when some envious clouds obscure the sun,
And mar that light reflected from his zone,
So thick'ning shadows cloud the mental ray,
When Disappointment makes the breast it's prey:
He's plac'd his talon'd finger on my heart,
And left a wound that ne'er shall cease to smart.

From Britain reft, beneath an eastern sun,
An exile's vagrant life I've now begun;

Torn from all those whom kindred claims endear,
Whom infant Nature taught me to revere :
Those whom affection solder'd to my breast ;
In whose fond arms I've oft-times been carest —
Why am I here, alas! Day glides on day,
In dull monotony they haste away :
No grateful change on Time's diurnal course ;
Hour succeeds hour, but often for the worse :
Still moping Melancholy spreads her wings,
And from the plumes a mental stupor flings.
When Time shall chase some twenty years away,
Should it be granted me to see the day
When Albion's vales shall greet my stranger'd eyes,
And free to breathe beneath my native skies,
Shall Happiness return ? A stranger I,
E'en where my voice first gave it's infant cry.
Just as the innocent, unconscious lamb —
Ere it has suck'd, sequester'd from the dam —
Knows not it's parent 'mongst the grazing tribe,
When strength of days permits it to imbibe
The meadow's offering : — alike is he,
Who from his country is induc'd to flee.
Returning, after twenty tedious years,
He knows no friends, long lodg'd in sepulchres,
In vain he seeks what he would wish to see,
For where's the search can pierce Eternity ?

If e'er again I traverse England's land,
My heart will instigate this quick demand —
" Where are my friends?" Truth whispers some are dead,
Aliens sprung up and living in their stead.
Some whom I left encircled in youth's zone,
Grown hoar, but wait Death's mandate to be gone;
Some who with me in boyhood sports had join'd,
Claim'd by stern Fate, have life's short boon resign'd:
Some few may be who wait upon the brow
Of Death's abyss, about to plunge below;
Sapp'd of youth's vigour, circumscrib'd by age,
Who had perform'd on life's eventful stage
A various part — now second childhood brings
The sithe of Death, to clip her drooping wings.
Where, then, may be the comrades of my youth?
Some dead — some scarr'd by Sorrow's sick'ning tooth —
All far dispers'd upon the world's wide bourne;
Most may have sped from whence there's no return.
Why will fond Mem'ry blissful scenes renew,
Whilst such forebodings clog the mental view?
Dearer than brother ! Lord of Heav'n forefend
That I should lose my schoolmate and my friend,
Before I quit this clime ! — May 't still be mine
To give my hand to feel the grasp of thine ! —
Well may I tremble ; twenty lagging years
May mock the stoutest nerve, and burthen youth with
       fears.

Tho' scarcely twenty moons have track'd their round,
Since last my footsteps kiss'd paternal ground,
Yet has Misfortune's thorn transpierc'd my breast—
Death's ta'en a father to his latest rest.
Now close enthrall'd within Earth's cloyless womb,
Succumb he lies, a vassal of the tomb:
Unsightly Grave! disgorge thy recent freight,
Restore my Parent to his mortal state;
Sunder thy cearments, give him from the dust—
—'Tis God rejects, and when was He unjust?

Scarce had I trod Ind's undelighting shore,
When Fame's trump clang'd—"Thy Parent is no more!"
The ceaseless buzz of Rumour caught my ear,
And drew abundant forth Affliction's tear.

Ah, my lov'd Sire! whose spirit wan'd away,
Far from thine home, to foreign suns a prey;
Just as prepar'd to cross the homeward wave,
Death snapp'd thy thread, and doom'd thee to the grave:
Still was thy lot far less severe than mine;
Thou'st bow'd submissive to the will Divine:
Whilst I have lost, whom—Heav'n forgive the sigh!—
None e'er can mate beneath this nether sky:

I've lost whom, tho' I knew not *, still was dear —
A Father, friend, — a friend the most sincere :
I knew the *name* of Father, but ne'er prest,
Who bore it lately, to my filial breast :
Just as my heart had kindled with desire
To view a no less lov'd, tho' unknown Sire,
Death stepp'd between the parent and his child,
Sunder'd the kindred link, and grimly smil'd :
Had'st thou ne'er left the land that gave thee life,
Thy parents, friends, thy children, and thy wife,
Thy child had never wail'd a Sire unknown,
Nor thou in stranger arms exhal'd Death's struggling
    groan.

How oft does Disappointment scowl on man!
But who shall compass Nature's future plan?
We build our hopes in air, and ev'ry frown
Of Disappointment hurls the fabric down :
He oft subverts the visionary fane;
Still Hope as quickly builds it up again :
But should Despair assail the fragile dome,
Th' illusive maiden bows her to the tomb :

* My father left England for India when I was but one year
old; I, in consequence, scarcely ever saw him ; and just as
I was preparing to go to him I heard of his death.

Born to beguile, she gives her fond caress,
And gulls the mind with *show* of happiness—
She whisper'd me, but told delusive lies.—
A fool ere while, I'm now at least more wise *.
To the C—D—T again awhile we'll turn,
In swift advancement tow'rds a drear sojourn.

Now at a distance seen, involv'd in haze,
The long sought region strikes upon the gaze :
Soon as arriv'd he's hurried to the land,
Unconscious whence proceeds the harsh command:
Guarded† he leaves the vessel's swelling side,
And the light shallop dashes thro' the tide ;

---

* This long digression may be considered as misplaced : but
as it contains reflections naturally arising from the subject, and
does not intrude upon any tale, I considered that it might be
appropriately introduced. The reflections on the death of my
parent may displease some who may happen to see this; yet I
trust, when it is known that I experienced a melancholy satisfaction in writing them, I shall stand excused.

† As soon as the India ships arrive, all the C—d—ts are forbidden to go on shore, until sent for by the commandant of the
C—d—t Establishment. A *sergeant* generally goes on board for
them with an order, and they are obliged to follow him like so
many recruits, being for the time under his absolute command :
he conducts them to the Establishment, where they are in-

The swarthy boatmen spread the flutt'ring sail,
Ply the swift oar, and catch the fav'ring gale:
Soon does the boat the distant landing reach,
And the glad stripling bounds upon the beach:
But, all bewilder'd, whither shall he hie?
Th' inquiring glance speaks eager from his eye;
Whilst he proceeds that *kind abode* to gain,
Where all who enter gnaw Restriction's chain;
Where each young soldier that arrives is sent —
The too well known C—D—T ESTABLISHMENT:
Where, clad in liv'ry, each unhappy wight
Drudges, for six dull months, from morn to night;
And — how the soul contemns the vile decree! —
Abridg'd of man's first, best immunity *.
Plac'd in this grand asylum — *sure 'tis kind* —
To learn to FIGHT, *to rectify the mind.*

Imagine one, who wears upon his cheek
Those growing marks which manhood's state bespeak;

stantly initiated; the rules, regulations, &c. are shown to them,
and after a day or two they enter upon their devoirs. The
restrictions are far greater than at any English boarding
school.

* Liberty is the highest privilege of man; which those who
enter this establishment are deprived of.

Whose ardent bosom constant swells elate,
With a high heart that prides to emulate ;—
Conceive him, just like bratling at a school,
MARSHALL'D each morning by some driv'ling fool ;
Tutor'd to march, to wheel, to dress, to halt,
Depress the shoulders, and the head exalt ;
To wear beneath the chin a round of leather,
Stiffen'd and rank, just fitted for a tether ;
To stand as prim as some tall straighten'd prop,
Fix'd in the ground to train the bending hop ;
Against the thighs the open palms to close,
And at the word turn out the flexile toes ;
T' extol the chin, and raise the weary eye,
As if to star-gaze o'er the spangled sky°;
Whilst some low sergeant vents the coarse reproof,
The strutting captain gazing far aloof,
And casting oft a fix'd determin'd eye,
To mark if any venture a reply :
Denied to answer, but oblig'd t' endure,
That to which Justice ought to grant a cure :—
But, when blind Ignorance usurps her crown,
She quits her seat and lays her balance down.

° Those C—d—ts whom I have ever had an opportunity of
viewing in this country, have been very often turned out to
drill before the stars have disappeared.

Is the young soldier honourably born,
To stand a butt for insolence and scorn?
Is he, whom Education has refin'd,
To bear the taunts that mark the menial mind?
Address'd to such should language be allow'd
As heard amongst the rabble of a crowd?
Or should a ribald sergeant basely dare
To ope his mouth, and insolently swear;
And menacing with imprecative speech,
Insult whom he was never form'd to teach?
Needless the questions—such has been the case,
And many are, who witness'd such disgrace*:
Oft, when th' unconscious slumb'ring world is still,
The new-form'd squad is hurried out to drill;
There forc'd in studied attitudes to stand,
And mark the tone decisive of command;
In doubtful balance on one foot to rest,
Those censur'd harsh who show themselves distrest;
Order'd one while to turn upon the heel,
To face, to march, to countermarch, to wheel;

* All this bears the stamp of truth. I have known a sergeant
who was appointed, at the C—d—t Establishment, to drill the
young men there, (and frequently too,) swear at some of them,
and make use of oaths disgraceful for gentlemen to hear. I
have also known the commandant mean enough to make use of
a vulgar and coarse execration.

Amid the march to make a sudden halt,
And then be lectur'd for some trivial fault,
Oblig'd to listen to each sharp rebuke,
Nor show annoyance even by a look;
Forbade to speak, to glance athwart the eye,.
Or e'en to gaze upon a passer by; '
But, like glued mummies, fix a vacant stare,
As if to *watch* the motion of the air*.
Oft have I seen when dews have drench'd the ground,
And chilly mists have cast their damps around,
The *awkicard squad*† parading to and fro,
Whilst the poor wretches shiver as they go;
Their heavy shoulders shrugg'd up to their ears,
And trickling down their cheeks the dewy tears;

---

* In that part of India where probably such a method would
be least expected to have been adopted, the C—d—t Establishment is nothing better, in point of regulation, than a common
soldier's barrack. All the young men are drilled, every morning, noon, and evening, by a sergeant and corporal, in the
presence of the captain commandant; and are put through all
the different exercises of private soldiers; and in a manner just
as harsh as private soldiers are generally treated.. How necessary all this may be I shall not attempt to decide: however, I
have heard many very old and respectable officers in India
ridicule it.

† The awkward squad is a party of the youngest recruits;
those who have just commenced drilling.

Wet to the skin, in most unseemly plight,.
Scarce pow'r to move or keep themselves upright;
Cramp'd with the cold*, which obstinately clung
Fast to those limbs on which the dew-drops hung ;
Four dreary hours paraded ev'ry day,
And with no other choice than to obey.

That this be needful I shall not dispute,
But is it meet th' instructor be a *brute?*

Suppose some man devoid of common sense,
Who yet to knowledge shows unjust pretence—
A man — to tutor well bred youths elect —
Mean in opinion, nor of thought correct,
A " fool of Nature," yet not void of art
To profit self, — the just man's *counterpart* —
Of grov'ling soul, of low and straiten'd mind,
Of feeling blunt, of manners unrefin'd ;
Wanting in education, meanly bred,
Aping the wit, yet little stor'd his head ;

---

* It may seem strange to say any thing of the cold of India :
but certain it is, that in some seasons, before sunrise, even in
the warmest latitudes, the cold is often piercing, particularly
when the dews fall, which they frequently do, and very
heavily.

Whose narrow heart's unravell'd in his face,
—A piece of human nature —in disgrace :
Haughty and servile where his int'rest tends,
Fawningly groveling to gain his ends : —
Suppose a man from low-born* parents sprung,
As gaudy flowers generate from dung ;
Whose scarlet trappings only would proclaim,
That he could boast a soldier's noble name ;
Who like some venal spy hears all you say,
Smiles to your face, then hurries to betray ;
Whose unregenerate mind is ever bent
On marring pleasure, pleas'd to circumvent ;
From one false hand throws friendship at your feet,
But in the other closely gripes Deceit.
Whilst specious smiles his countenance invest,
Oft ambush'd hatred rankles in his breast :
Like the keen lynx he watches thro' the day,
To spring upon some unsuspecting prey :

* It must be ever allowed ungenerous to despise any person
on account of his low parentage : but where any man so far
forgets his mean descent as to arrogate to himself a pride or
superciliousness, which he can have no right to display, he
immediately forfeits all claim to respect and delicacy from
another.

And should he fail, in base expedients wise,
To gain his end, the meanest arts he tries.
'Tis when his victim deems him most secure,
That he contrives to draw him to his lure ;
Disarms Suspicion by his double smile,
And acts the crafty, treach'rous crocodile.

　　When some poor youth, by wiles at length deceiv'd,
Thinks him too honest to be disbeliev'd ;
He takes advantage of the stripling's thought,
And quick invites him to the enliv'ning draught ;
By covert questions * lab'ring hard to find,
Each turn, each fav'rite bias of his mind :
And should success attend his vile essays,
He grasps the profit and his pow'r displays ;
Decries the man from whom by chance he drew
Things scarcely known, or only known to few ;
Grins o'er his foul deceit, and subt'ley tries
To injure merit by insidious lies.

　　* This alludes to a custom adopted by a certain commandant
of a C—d—t Establishment, which was, of gaining information of
the most secret occurrences which had place among the young
men, by putting indirect questions to the more dull and un-
guarded, and thereby often collecting much more than the
persons questioned meant to reveal.

Imagine such appointed to command
Youths proudly born, and no ignoble band,
Whose gen'rous bosoms swell with hopes of Fame,
And to the *genuine soldier* yield acclaim.

How must each lib'ral soul indignant scorn
A dull Jackdaw, whom peacock plumes adorn!
Such, too, their tutor in that glorious art,
Which fires with zeal the emulative heart;
Points to that fane where sov'reign Glory rears
Her golden wand, and checks more recreant fears;
Shoots thro' each vein that warms the mortal frame,
An ardent fire that glows with ceaseless flame.

What an instructor! Like a painted fly,
Ere while a grub, he sports his gaudy die,
Twirls round his cane and cocks his old chapeau,
And, prone to folly, apes the simp'ring beau;
With self-important glance erects his head,
Like some rude statue's, form'd of pond'rous lead:
Grinning approval, oft he rears his glass,
And, tho' unconscious, shows himself an ass;
Struts off with belted sabre to parade,
Like some round butcher at a masquerade.—

Thus dung-fed insects that from filth begun, -
Spread their fine wings and flutter to the sun *.

Ye who now groan beneath the galling rule
Of one who wears the badge at least of fool,
Ere ye arriv'd on India's trackless waste,
Had ye the slightest thought to be disgrac'd?
Why did ye quit a kind, indulgent home,
And challenge sad vicissitudes to come?
May your experience make hereafter wise
All who would speculate 'neath Indian skies.

Here shall my muse, in Truth's unborrow'd dress,
A few important incidents express.

Conceive the sequent orders put in force,
A check to Freedom's unpolluted course;
A base infringement on man's noblest laws,
Where Freedom gains his best deserv'd applause.

To each C—D—T, when having giv'n his name,
He's rank'd among the training sons of Fame: —

* " Thus morning insects, that from muck begun,
" Shine, buzz, and fly-blow, in the setting sun."
POPE.

Suppose these paltry regulations sent,
As standing orders of th' Establishment.
But (nor conceive I'm fabricating lies)
Ere I commence, 'tis meet that I premise,
First he's requir'd to give a just account
Of all his property, and state th' amount;
Told how he ought to spend it, when and where;
That he'd best trust it to the Captain's * care;
Who, kindly cautious, will take proper heed
That it shall ne'er be spent but when there's need.
—Too gen'rous man! How is it he's so kind?—
Gold's the sole magnet that attracts his mind.
Now each his age is order'd to declare;
Penn'd instant down with circumspective care;
Then, in succession, each attending wight
Stands 'neath a frame, that ascertains his height.

The Captain now is careful to supply
What he conceives the stripling ought to buy;
Spoons †, knives and forks, plates, table, chair and cot,
Cups, saucers, dishes, and I know not what:

* A captain commanded the C—d—t Establishment.
† Upon the arrival of each person, every thing considered
necessary by the commandant is provided; and those to whom
it is offered are obliged to purchase it, however they may be

Much cheaper, too, he fails not to declare,
And better far, than can be bought elsewhere.
Should any one by chance refuse to take 'em,
He stamps and roars, and swears by G—d he'll make 'em.

Here follow now the *rules*, all mean at best:
The simplest I'll select, and leave the rest.

At ev'ry meal each member *must* attend,
Nor dare invite or relative or friend;
Lest such his tender morals should debase,
Lead him astray, or tempt him to disgrace:
A childish, trifling, academic rule,
Which merits well the gibe of ridicule.
'Tis strictly order'd next, that each C—D—T
Shall ne'er take off his belt or bayonet,
But in important cases, such as when
Sleep casts his fetters o'er the sons of men;

disposed to the contrary; and the things thus provided are
generally made, as were Dr. Wolcott's razor-seller's goods—
to sell only, without regard to strength or worth in the manu-
facture. I knew a young man who refused to take the things
thus provided, but met with reproach for his presumption, as
it was considered; and was obliged to take them at last,
although he had purchased what he wanted elsewhere.

Or when the rattling drum and fife's shrill cry,
Announce the moment of refection nigh.
No one's allow'd to entertain a guest;
Or should he dare, must suffer from arrest:
No money is permitted to be spent
In food superfluous *; sign of discontent:
'Tis also will'd that none shall harbour friends;
And all no doubt for wise and wond'rous ends:
Wondrous they may be, but that they are wise
Candour disowns, and sound good sense denies.

Such as, without a murmur, prompt obey,
Nor from these orders turn their minds away,
Are well rewarded; for, wedg'd side by side,
In *one horse chay*, with Captain QUIRK *they ride.*

Now must none dine from their establish'd mess;
A *rule so just* 'twere madness to transgress:
For who offend in this are doubly base,
It leaves a blot which nought shall e'er erase;
And once convicted of such profanation,
Nought from arrest can serve as a salvation.

* It is a strict order, that no one shall have eating parties
in his tent. A young man who bought a ham, was repri-
manded for having laid out his money on *superfluous* food.

No one can dare be absent after three,
Hour for parade; from thence must all to tea;
Nor can a single soul the while presume,
Without the Captain's leave, to quit the room.

    Oblig'd are all, to hinder them from play,
To go to school for three dull hours each day:
Safe under sturdy lock and key • confin'd;
Purpose august! to *decorate* the mind;
Whilst the grave Captain gives the frequent look,
To see that no one gazes off his book:
Should he detect an idler, with a frown
He calls for pen and ink, and marks him down;
Sends to the G-n-r-l his poor complaint,
Whilst he—in sooth by far more man than saint—
Indites some churlish censure; joy the while
Tort'ring his rigid muscles to a smile.
Thus perfectly they understand each other,
For ev'ry mongrel is a mongrel's brother.

    Such is the life C—D—TS are doom'd to lead,
'Gainst which unbiass'd Justice ought to plead:—
But, hold awhile, I'd quite forgot to say,
That Sunday is their only holyday.

           • An absolute fact.

For then are all exempted from parade,
And sent to church, in comic garb array'd ;
White trowsers, gaiters delicately fine,
A vest that reaches just where ends the spine;
Upon the head a cap with tow'ring feather,
That waves about and frolics with the weather;
Across the back and breast a belt is thrown,
From which a bayonet hangs graceful down:
And over all a silken sash is tied,
With two large horse knots* dangling at the side :
Under the chin, as British bull-dogs wear,
A collar's plac'd, to fix the nose in air,
Compos'd of leather, thick with black-ball grim'd,
And by a daily blacking-brush sublim'd.
Thus habited each stripling goes to pray,
And reverently hails the Sabbath day:
For after pray'rs, with Captain QUIRK's consent,
Some are allow'd to leave th' Establishment;
But only such as scorning honest sport,
Have shown a conduct late of good report :
E'en these — so rare th' indulgences bestow'd —
Have, for enjoyment, but few hours allow'd ;
For at the hour of nine a watch goes round,
To see that each within his tent be found ;

* Such as are seen at cart horses' tails.

And, any absent at that prudent time,
Some *awful* punishment awaits the crime.
Thus like young puppies, some old maiden's care,
They're once a week allow'd — to take the air*.
What heart that glows with Pride's unblemish'd fires,
When foster'd from the spring of pure desires—
What soul that soars on Freedom's genial wing,
Could feel such trammels without murmuring;
Would tamely bear it's spirit trampled down,
Or brook unjust Oppression's recreant frown;
Hear the imperious slur from Power's tongue,
And forc'd to silence, meanly stoop to wrong:
Forbade to contradict, whilst ev'ry lie
Jostles 'gainst truth †, and gains it's victory!

---

* All the rules and regulations touched on in the above, are
exactly as they do, or at least *did*, exist at the C—d—t Establishment.

† False representations from the C—m—d—t have been frequently listened to and obtained credit, when honest truth in
defence has been given unheard, or suffer̜d defeat.

END OF THE SECOND PART.

THE CADET.

Part the Third.

.........." Thus with the year
" Seasons return: but not to me returns
" Day, or the sweet approach of even or morn."
                                        MILTON.

" Faciam ut hujus loci semper meminris."—TERENCE.

WHERE lives the man, who nourish'd at the springs
Where matron Science dips her hallow'd wings,
Would tamely bend beneath oppressive rule,
And learn the task in Folly's baser school?
Where lives the man of highly temper'd mind,
Would at Oppression's footstool crouch resign'd;

Look on the scourge and tamely bear the smart;
Nor act, when injur'd, a defensive part?
Who, that could Envy's smile malignant mark,
— A monstrous hag that murders in the dark, —
Would for a moment pause, in her despight,
To drag the filthy monster to the light;
Tear off the tatters that conceal her frame,
And on her carcass stamp her cursed name?
But there be many frequent giv'n to pain,
And doom'd to tug at Persecution's chain;
Depriv'd the pow'r—Is such privation just?—
To strike the proud insulter to the dust.

Ye Afric tribes! ye nations born to be
Drudges to man, poor sons of Slavery;
Fated Affliction's fiercest pangs to feel,
To court life only for your masters' weal:
Valued as beasts of burthen, bought and sold;
Born but to curse the baleful pow'r of gold;
Oft forc'd to fatten with your sweat the land,
Life's thread spun out by Labour's drudging hand:—
How should Humanity that trade despise,
Which works for you such mournful miseries?
Whilst Heav'n's o'erpotent regent chaps the soil,
Chain'd to the pond'rous sledge, o'erspent with toil;

And the sharp lash at intervals applied,
Where strength exhausts and vigour is denied.
Still, tho' the keenest woes your lives assail,
Such as no earthly joys can countervail,
Oft have I heard Mirth's gratifying song,
And sprightly sallies sport upon the tongue:
Oft have I seen ye join the festive game,
Twang the Jew's harp, or dance around the flame;
Clasp your fond dingy partners in your arms,
Smack their thick lips, unheeding future harms*.

* There is no doubt but that slavery must be the most
miserable state that can fall to the lot of man. However,
they who are born to this cannot certainly feel it so sensibly
as those who are reduced to that situation after they have
known the blessings of liberty: to the former, it becomes a
kind of second nature, but the latter never can be reconciled
to it. I have seen so much of either real or apparent happiness among the slaves at the Isle of France, that I have been
frequently inclined to believe that many Christians, living too
in the very spot where freedom is said to hold her favourite
seat, enjoy less of that placid content and substantial joy, that
undisturbed placidity of mind, and tranquillity of conscience,
which is so often manifestly conspicuous among these despised
sons of nature. It afforded me much of satisfaction to see that
the slaves at the Isle of France are, for the most part, very
humanely treated.

Your labour sure is lightsome, when compar'd
To his who Freedom's noblest joys has shar'd :
Then, sport of fickle Fortune, doom'd to feel
The keenest woes that issue from her wheel :
Fated to feel Oppression's rankling goad,
And, unrequited, bear it's heaviest load ;
His lofty spirit humbled to the dust,
No friend to shield him from Misfortune's gust ;
Whilst some insulter scoffs his hapless state,
And thus augments the weight of galling Fate.
Those who have drank at Freedom's limpid streams,
Tasted her joys and sported in her beams ;
When stern Restriction, with uncourtly voice,
Bawls hoarsely loud, and bids them not rejoice :
Then, too susceptive of Affliction's throes,
If brought to bend, they clamour at their woes :
Their free-born hearts contemn a galling chain,
Swell with just scorn, and spurn the abject pain.

And shall a Briton tamely undergo
A Dastard's thrall, effeminating wo !
Shall one of free-form'd spirit tamely bear
The bitter censure and the taunt severe ?
Who that would truckle to a dunghil threat,
Or at a snarler's saucy stare retreat ?

Who'd bear the coarse revilings of a tongue,
Whence nothing falls but Reason's very *dung**;
Which seldom stirs but when it is to blame,
Like some old harridan's long dead to shame?

Don't harmless worms, which after death despoil
The mortal relic, trodden on, recoil?
Does not the bee, that " toils each shining hour,"
Sting the rash hand that plucks it from the flow'r?
Does not the ant, when with unjust delight
'Tis taken and tormented, strive to bite?
Instinct instructs the reptile to defence,
And to chastise unworthy violence;
Then should bright Reason prompt the nobler mind
To spurn the Tyrant, and contemn his kind.

What more repugnant than enforc'd to be
The tame spectator of Hypocrisy;
Nor dare unmask the monster to the light,
Hid by the cloak of Pow'r from public sight?
What worse than, 'gainst the will, compell'd to own
The waspish influence of a senseless drone;

* I hope it does not militate against good sense to class
indelicate language and ignorant expression as the dung of
reason.

Who scoffs at all that's more supremely good,
Whilst ev'ry meanness circles with his blood?

　　It hath been said — how vast a work is man!
The proudest ornament in Nature's plan!
Of wondrous faculty, of sense refin'd,
And, next to angels, of exalted mind!
Yet observation oftentimes may prove,
That from the ape he's scarcely one remove;
And oft the beams of soul so faintly shine,
That scarce he seems the work of hands Divine:
Still there are times when man supremely tow'rs,
And almost claims a rank with godlike pow'rs.

　　Oh! India, boundless nursery of ills,
Where Sorrow's stagnant fountain constant fills;
The more mine eyes thy boundless realms survey,
The more does Grief his fretting pow'r display.
England! blest Isle! oft Mem'ry clings to thee,
And draws thy scenes of young felicity;
When, hours of study o'er, I blithly hied
To catch the trout, along the streamlet's side:
Where, oft recumbent on the tufted green,
And gazing on the still, delighting scene,
Imagination would her wings display,
Hover awhile, then raptur'd soar away;

Till—like the spark that's swallow'd in the blaze—
Lost at the last in Thought's involving maze.

Then, as in Boyhood's animating prime
I onward sped, nor mark'd the course of Time,
What sweet communion have I held with thee,
Kindest companion*! friend of first degree!
When, from the school released, look'd arm-in-arm,
We stroll'd along, with mutual fondness warm;
Our hopes, our fears, reciprocally told,
And joy'd our dearest wishes to unfold!

Friend and companion of my earliest years!
The loss of thee draws forth my bitt'rest tears;
For here, of thee, no semblance can I find,
Of thee so good, so estimably kind;
So free from guile, of heart so gently mild,
Nature may claim thee as her worthiest child.

England! how oft, when strolling thro' thy fields,
Where graceful Harvest her abundance yields,
Reflection, mother of sublime delight,
Has giv'n Earth's choicest beauties to my sight;

* My estimable friend and school-fellow, Mr. J. Windeatt.

And strongly pictur'd to my youthful mind
Those variqus wonders which have aw'd mankind.
The vegetative world, the structure man,
The spangled arch of Heav'n, stupendous plan!
The central sun, the mazes of the sky,
The mighty Ocean's vast profundity;
The stars * that in such even tenor roll,
Creation's vast, inestimable whole :—
These, as thought undisturb'd has taken wing,
And all around me glow'd the tints of Spring;
Have op'd mine eyes to his amazing pow'r,
Who rides the storm and bids the tempests low'r;
Who sends the bolted light'ning from on high,
And speaks in awful thunders from the sky.

How diff'rent here my unbefriended state!
Corrosive Sorrow triumphs o'er my fate :
No genial recreations can be found,
To chase the clouds that hang the heart around;
No kind companion, on whose honest breast
I might recline mine aching head to rest!
Here ev'ry wound inflicted on the mind
Does but recall the joys I left behind;

* It is scarcely necessary to say, that this cannot allude to the *fixed* stars, but to the planets.

Clears Recollection's optic, and displays
The sportive pastimes of mine infant days.

In those most happy hours, for ever gone,
When uncloy'd Peace stood forth and hail'd me son,
Oft have I join'd the healthful festive play,
Whilst pass'd the hours unwittingly away ;
And, mix'd with social comrades, cheerly spent
Days, weeks, and months, in unalloy'd content.
But, cruel change ! since first I view'd this clime,
Sorrow has brooded on the wings of Time.

My Country ! sadly now the hour I mourn,
When first I left thy sea-encircling bourn ;
Left all I held most eminently dear,
To wander sad and discontented here.
Tho' here stern Winter never dare to frown,
And Summer wears an everlasting crown,
Still would I rather brave December snows,
When the north wind his freezing terrors blows ;
When ice binds fast the earth in glitt'ring mail,
And falling clouds descend in rattling hail ;
Than, sooth'd by lux'ry, live in savage realms,
Where gloomy care the sadden'd heart o'erwhelms ;

Where Friendship never lifts a shielding arm
To baffle wo, to ward the strokes of harm *.
In Albion's vales, beneath a freezing sky,
When all was hoar from Winter's tyranny;
Oft have I sallied forth, a stripling wight,
My youthful bosom heaving with delight,
Arm'd with my gun, to shoot the crippled thrush,
Batter'd each hedge, and pelted ev'ry bush;
Then creeping cautious on my torpid game,
Levell'd the death-fraught tube with doubtful aim,
Eager to kill; and if I did succeed,
Hied me quick home to tell the wondrous deed:
Upon the board, as proof of early skill,
Display'd what chance assisted me to kill.
Such were benignant moments; happy days!
For ever lost in Time's involving maze.

* That friendship is so rarely to be met with in India, as
hinted at above, many, probably, who have spent much of their
time there may be inclined to dispute: however, this I can
positively assert, that no death takes place amongst the Europeans in this country, but it affords, if a partial satisfaction
with respect to the community at large, still a very visible
satisfaction to a great number; for in the civil service it leaves
an opening to be filled up, and in the military it is equally an
advantage to all who gape for promotion.

Oft I remind me when at Even's close,
The shrilly warblers sinking to repose,
And Sol, restricted of his beams, illum'd
The liquid mirror, and the clouds assum'd
A fiery radiance, all grotesquely pil'd
In antic forms, magnificently wild;—
When the breeze, slumb'ring on the placid bay,
Presag'd a peaceful closing to the day;
And on the surface of the dimpling wave*
The freighted boats their pointed bosoms lave;
Scar the smooth surface, scud before the wind,
And leave a lengthen'd trail of foam behind.
Oft was I wont in museful mood to rove,
With one † whom ties of Nature bade me love;
When Eve's soft zephyrs gave the faint perfume
Of various flow'rs, conceal'd amid the gloom;—
When dimming twilight dropt her dusky veil,
And light o'erpow'r'd at length, began to fail,
Long would we muse upon the scene around,
As Silence reign'd in solitude profound;

* I was born on the banks of the Dart; perhaps one of the
most beautiful rivers in England, although not generally ranked
as such. The spot where I first beheld the light, is, I can con-
scientiously declare, the most beautiful that ever came under
my observation.   † My sister.

Converse of present bliss, of future joy,
Of days escap'd, untarnish'd by alloy;
Build unsubstantial schemes of future weal,
Reckless what haps we might be doom'd to feel;
And as we stroll'd the rising hills along,
Oft rest to hear the ploughman's homeward song;
Muse on the humbler happiness of those,
Whose daily toils insure the best repose:
Dwell, fondly dwell on speculative themes,
And fancy bliss in all our infant dreams:
Pour forth our mutual thoughts; and oft, the while,
Give interchange of fond Affection's smile:
Then, as the moon began to pierce the gloom,
And countless stars begem'd th' o'erarching dome;
Clothing the silent world in vestal light,
And giving graceful beauties to the night;
Frequent we'd ponder on the ambient scene,
As o'er us stole Contentment's sweet serene;
Gaze on the mighty wonders hung on high,
Those countless suns that light the waste of sky;
That occupy such vast extent of place;
Yet all mere atoms in the womb of space;
Converse of Him, whose omnipresent eye
Can dart thro' worlds, and all their works espy;
Pass the swift hours in profitable talk,
Scarce mindful of the distance of our walk;

'Till Ev'ning's chilly dews began to fall,
And the bell slowly warn'd us to the hall.
There seated round the animating fire,
Long would we dwell on what we lov'd t' admire;
And, whilst the smile of approbation threw
Joy on each cheek, and on each visage grew;
Recount the wanton tricks of earlier days,
When harmless follies ever had their praise;
When truant sport engross'd the easy mind,
And thought was changeful as th' autumnal wind.
If Peace was ever inmate of the breast,
In that delightful season 'twas possest:
Light was the heart, by sorrow unassail'd,
When inoffensive Innocence prevail'd :—
Encompass'd round by those whom we adore,
What can the restless mortal covet more?
Oh! how the social circle us'd to charm,
Expand the soul, the kindred bosom warm!
There more than Father,—Uncle,—Guardian, Friend,
Who hast a heart perfection scarce could mend;
Have I from thee imbib'd the precept wise,
And learnt the fadeless charms of lore to prize,
I've listen'd oft to thy preceptive tongue,
On which so sweetly Wisdom's accents hung:
Stor'd from thy mouth that nourishment refin'd,
Which serves for food and polish to the mind:

Leads it, thro' life, to search that blest abode,
Where dwell the just — the bosom of our God.

Yes, valued Uncle! 'tis to thee I owe,
If not the whole, yet most of what I know;
For in gay Boyhood's more unmindful hour,
Ere well acquaint with Wisdom's brighter pow'r;
When sprightly pastimes all my soul engrost,
All serious thought in light amusement lost;
I smil'd on Idleness, I woo'd, caress'd,
And in mine arms the vacant monster press'd;
'Till thou did'st ope the hidden stores of thought,
And to mine aid the pow'rs of Reason brought.

Too fond remembrance! why those scenes renew?
Why crowd such magic pictures on my view?
Why give such aggravation to the grief
From which my heart can now find no relief?
Vain my lament, 'twill never more be giv'n,
(O falsify the dread prognostic, Heav'n!)
Again to view my home, thus moaning fear,
Whilst throbs my bosom, whispers to my ear:

Inhospitable region! India, why
Did'st thou entice me 'neath thy fiercer sky?

Why did I Britain's greener vallies leave,
And my late placid heart of peace bereave?
The die is cast, and useless 'tis to mourn,
Since vain are all my wishes to return.
But am I single? No.— How many more
Have left their homes for this ill-omen'd shore!

Misguided youths! how came ye first to roam
Far from a welcome and protecting home?
To learn the lesson which Experience gives,
That he's most happy, who contented lives,
Nor cares to wander. Had ye known ere while
Those fraudful fallacies, which oft beguile
Whom Prudence sways not, ye had never felt
The galling strokes by sore Affliction dealt,
Ne'er left the land where all those blessings live
That independent liberty can give.

Man, hing'd to folly! when will he be wise?
'Tis he engenders all his miseries;
Hews out, too oft, some track, which, if he tread,
Wo shakes her scourge and settles on his head.
How oft, by Hope's delusive voice beguil'd,
Like a light rattle that decoys a child,
He hurries onward, heedless of the way,
Till at the last he falls Destruction's prey!

Ye who by lying Rumour's tongue misled,
Seek Ind for wealth, tho' scarce 'twill yield ye bread;
Soon as your feet these torrid regions press,
Ye taste the mingled chalice of Distress;
Are plac'd beneath the guidance of a man,
Form'd, one would deem, by "Nature's journeyman:"—
If it *be* not, at least it *may* be so,
Ye're given to taste of many a minor wo;
Compell'd to stoop to insult, and receive
Each base abuse which Insolence shall give;
To hear, and bear unansw'ring, many a curse,
Nor dare resent, lest ye experience worse:
By watchful spies surrounded thro' the day,
To mark or what ye do or what ye say;
Each rude expression noted which they hear,
And instant giv'n to their employer's ear;
Who, on malicious purpose ever bent,
Joys to essay the goad of punishment.

None but the recreant lifts Oppression's hand
At those subjected to unjust command:
He who can boast a truly noble soul,
Inspires esteem whilst bending to controul: —
Where gen'rous minds possess ascendant sway,
They call forth love, nor e'er that love bewray.

Like the byæna, prowling thro' the wood,
Or the false crocodile, athirst for blood,
Is he who takes advantage of his pow'r,
Cramps the fresh bud, or crops the embryo flow'r;
Gores the young bosom with a searching wound,
And hurls the props of honour to the ground : —
Yea worse, far worse; by Heav'n's superior will,
Beast lives on beast —'tis Nature bids them kill;
'Twixt Good and Evil they no diff'rence find : —
Can such excuse be pleaded by mankind ?
Still are there many, *some* there be at least,
More fierce, more savage than th' Hyrcanean beast;
Who, tho' they kill not, plant the stings of pain,
And tighten Care's interminable chain.
Many there are who mock Compassion's moan,
And smile to hear Distress's heavy groan :
To them no higher joy than to molest,
And pluck the cherub Comfort from the breast.
Nor single he, who has disgrac'd my strain,
In other breasts tyrannic feelings reign : —
Yes, — *some* who boast them an exalted name,
Are not exempt from failings much the same
As his; who, with the meanest rabble bred,
Tamper'd with Fortune 'till she crown'd his head :
—He's now a rod, which *Pow'r* too frequent takes;
And, truth must own, a *bitter rod he makes.*

Oh! ye who loll upon the couch of ease,
Nor aught acquainted with the mind's disease,
Free from those trammels which oppress the soul,
When straining 'neath the shackles of controul,
Deem how severe his melancholy lot,
Who's forc'd to act as will directs him not;
Urg'd by the goad of overbearing pow'r,
(As bends the ruffian blast the fragile flow'r,)
To yield, coerc'd, to mercenary thrall,
Bend at a beck, nor fail a tyrant's call;
Oblig'd to stoop to despicable sway,
And view an upstart brave the face of day;
Denied to act as feelings would be prone,
And scarce one moment of the day his own.

Ye who commix in Freedom's jovial throng,
Pause on those troubles which compose my song;
Beseech the Goddess, at whose shrine ye bend,
T' extend her arm — the injur'd cause befriend!
Arise ye sons of Liberty: pursue,
With honest wrath, Oppression's dastard crew:
Prone to the dust be all her standards hurl'd,
" Her name, her nature, wither'd from the world."

But now, desponding Muse, thy theme pursue,
And mark those scenes which crowd upon thy view;

Give to the world, what yet it scarcely knows,
The life of the C—D—T, with it's attendant woes.

Conceive the youth now nigh to be remov'd
From that asylum which he never lov'd:
Pleasure, sometime unfelt, dilates his heart,
And thoughts of Freedom heal Restriction's smart;
New generated hopes his breast assail,
And blessings seem to float on Fancy's gale;
He counts the moments of the hast'ning day,
And deems each moment tardy on it's way;
Pants for that eager season to arrive,
When smiling Liberty her joys shall give.

Tho' once deceiv'd, Experience still is young;
Nor becomes sage till taught by frequent wrong;
Hope will exist, in spite of ev'ry pain,
And, oft destroy'd, as often lives again;
Spreads her bright flutt'ring pinions o'er the head,
Nor is Grief cureless until Hope be fled.

As when some pretty chorister confin'd,
Escapes his cage and skims along the wind,
Settles o'erjoy'd upon some limed spray,
And, freed from one, becomes another's prey:

So the C—D—T, from one oppressor free,
May feel again the yoke of Tyranny;
Escape one man's effeminating thrall,
And in some other's unsuspecting fall.

Now to my gloomy theme. C—D—T no more,
With heart elate, he joins his destin'd *corps*,
Thinking that all his sorrows here shall end,
And Peace, with future joys, her blessings blend.

Where now those hopes his vagrant fancy fed?
Resolv'd to that from whence they first were bred!
Here does he find his happiness complete?
His dreams are baffled and endure defeat;
For many a sad and unexpected ill,
With sullen discontent, pursues him still.

Plac'd 'neath some haughty, ignorant command*,
Where Pow'r uprears Presumption's daring land,
Where haughty pride, with arrogance combin'd,
Extends his empire o'er th' ungenerous mind;

* I am thus far happy in being placed under a kind commanding officer: but many are there far less fortunate, who are exposed to all the tyranny which superior rank gives an opportunity of exercising.

Where Rank, that covert to the soul that's base,
Scoffs at what's just, protected from disgrace—
He's forc'd to crouch submissive to their sway;
His only choice to listen and obey.

Let Freedom's children pause and yield the sigh,
Nor think the soldier free from misery!
Deem'd independant—Ah, what error's there!
The slave 's, if not from toil, more free from care:
Nor might the proudest mind disdain to own
The lash more lenient than the tyrant's frown.
Few, I can boldly venture to aver,
Live more dependant than an officer:
For all of higher rank, if any say
Do this or that, he cannot but obey.
Oft have I seen, with pageant rank endued,
Some sniv'lling recreant fire his lagging blood;
And, 'neath the pompous covert of a name,
O'er some pure bosom cast the soil of shame.
—So may the chatt'ring magpie — *in his cage*—
Dare with impunity the eagle's rage.

Behold the gen'rous youth, of spirit proud,
Whose nobler nature marks him from the crowd,
Too indiscreetly eager to explore
The fancied treasures of this faithless shore—

Behold him, just in Manhood's earlier dawn,
When Mirth unfetter'd stamps him for her own;
Leave all he loves for speculative bliss,
Which Expectation whispers may be his.

From School's unpleasant bonds but just releas'd,
And deeming Boyhood's trifling hours * have ceas'd,
He quits his home for Ind's destructive clime,
And casts a load upon the wings of Time;
For Wo assails, and as years onward roll,
Steeps each sad moment in his pois'nous bowl;
Nor long when once he treads this treach'rous coast,
Ere he perceives his peace, his comfort lost;
Days upon days in dull succession glide,
But flow unmourn'd on Time's eventful tide;
From home sequester'd, no perspective cheers,
No ray of future happiness appears;
The heavy hours in one dull tenour run,
Each has it's end, the same as it begun:
Weeks, months, and seasons, speed in dull career,
But life's dark prospect still continues drear;

* We very commonly find that young persons are delighted when they fancy the era of boyhood elapsed, although confessedly the happiest season of human existence, from the vain and ridiculous wish to be men.

The bitter cup of Sorrow daily fills,
And pours abundant forth it's pungent ills*.

First the young Stripling, by his hopes beguil'd,
Contented lands on Asia's sun-scorch'd wild:
But soon are all his ardent wishes marr'd,
And from expected ease his soul debarr'd:
Soon the light fabrics of his mind decay,
And like the mists of morning glide away;
So shall this world in after-times dissolve,
And all it's products in the wreck involve.

Suppose the youth, his first rude bondage† o'er,
Appointed Ensign to some native corps;
Conceive a few dull months, a twelvemonth past,
And mark th' enjoyment he procures at last.
In sullen discontent the weeks pass on,
And Melancholy hails him as her son:
Reflection, pointing to his natal isle,
O'ercasts his brow and robs Contentment's smile:

* I cannot presume to say that living in India would operate
on every young man's mind as suggested above: however, I can
be justified in saying, that it may on some; and few certainly
appear contented.

† This alludes to his release from the C—d—t Establishment.

Seldom a bright'ning moment intervenes
To chase the gloom of life's unvarying scenes;
To mild Seclusion's silent bow'r he goes,
And, hid from riot, tries to seek repose:
Still restless discontent assails him there,
And stirs up the disquietudes of care.

He views those comrades with disdainful eyes,
(Prone to excess,) and from their presence flies;
For Dissipation here supremely reigns,
Saps hardy life, and riots in the veins*.

Distress'd unfortunate! as years revolve,
No joys his heart from goading pains absolve;
His spirit crush'd by tyrannizing sway,
To Apathy a voluntary prey;
Each tardy day on leaden pinions flies,
Mark'd but by Sorrow's too oppressive sighs.

Ask ye the cause? Then thus is the reply,
The cause is glanc'd from Pow'r's presumptuous eye:

* The dissipated mode of life in India has been glanced
at before; but I would still take this opportunity of declaring,
that I do not believe there is any other country where excess
is so fatally encouraged.

When that rough monster rears his pageant crest,
And swells to arrogance his speckled breast,
What, as his speech, can so severely pain,
That heart where Pride has not forsook his reign ;
Where Honour triumphs ?—Thou, unhappy youth,
May'st oft have prov'd this melancholy truth.

Plac'd 'neath some senseless Dolt's * severe command,
Who grasps the scourge of Rigour in his hand ;
Scoffs at the nicer feelings of the soul,
And makes his crest the rod of low Controul ;
Who prides in venting undeserv'd rebuke;
Yet fears opposing Honour's dauntless look ;
A tyrant 'neath the gilded cloak of pow'r,
A trembling recreant in danger's hour;
Who aims the shafts, on any slight pretence,
Of angry Censure against Innocence ;
Casts on the man malevolent disgrace,
Whom he would fear encount'ring face to face—

* This picture is taken from nature. I am not familiarly
acquainted with the person who is the subject of it, nor did I
ever speak to him, therefore the above could not have been
written from prejudice; but I have frequently seen him in his
military capacity, and heard his manner of treating inferior
officers. No one who has served under him will find the above
draught, I may venture to assert, too glowing.

Plac'd beneath such, what mortal could employ
The hours of life in unrestricted joy !
Plac'd beneath such, all happiness must flee,
And substitute it's adverse—Misery.

Is this the sum of all thy suff'rings? No !
It forms not e'en a moiety of thy wo ;
Here cares eternal live, few joys are known,
For scarce is unsubstantial life thine own.

Why then will parents be so falsely wise
To send their sons to scorch 'neath torrid skies?
Fated to groan a weary length of years,
Far from their homes, from all the heart reveres.

Here for a while the Muse would check her wing,
Tho' soon again to strike a plaintive string.

END OF THE THIRD PART.

THE CADET.

Part the Fourth.

"O ye woods, spread your branches apace;
"To your deepest recesses I fly;
"I would hide with the beasts of the chase;
"I would vanish from every eye."

SHENSTONE.

. . . ." Ore, misere laborum
"Tantorum, miserere animæ non digna ferentis."

VIRGIL.

To thee, for whom commenc'd the mournful song,
The Muse would still awhile her notes prolong;
Explore thy chart of life, and give to view
What frequent woes thy sad career pursue.

Oft, when War's clarion hurtles thro' the air,
And thou art doom'd it's vast fatigues to bear;

When marching o'er a savage hostile soil,
Where robbers* swarm, and live on lawless spoil:
Where oft the lonely traveller's misled,
Stripp'd of his stores, then rifled of his head;
Where nought's secure from that abandon'd brood,
Who feed on what they can obtain by blood;
Who, in vast swarms assembled, scour the fields,
Existing sole on what their pillage yields: —
Oft are thy chattels † ta'en before thine eyes,
All that thou hast the ruthless spoiler's prize;

* The province of Guzzerat is partly populated by a cast of
men whom they call (as well as I can adapt the word to
English orthography) Bheels : they are, probably, as desperate
robbers as can be found on the whole continent of Asia. They
plunder in considerable parties, and their principal weapon is
the bow and arrow. I once heard a circumstance related of
three of these robbers entering a tent that was guarded by six
sentinels; the whole six receiving an arrow each at the same
moment. The plunderers entered,. and took what they could
hastily lay their hands on; then gave themselves regress by
slitting down the canvass of the tent. On entering a room
where a person happens to be in bed, one of the ruffian party
generally places himself at the side of the bed, with a dagger
ready drawn, to put the unfortunate person to death if he
should chance to awake.

† Officers are very frequently robbed in this country.

Clothes, money, all thy scant domestic store,
Stol'n from thee — now to be redeem'd no more;
Not left thee e'en the little lowly bed,
Where thou wert wont to rest thine aching head;
Nor wherewithal thy losses to repair,
Or shield thy bosom from the gripe of care;
But, unbefriended, left to feel the smart,
That adverse chance essays upon the heart.

Now hemm'd by Poverty — severest curse!
Thy monthly pittance ravish'd from thy purse;
Art thou, disastrous fortune! — doom'd to try
Thy credit with the sons of usury *;
Oblig'd, however galling, to endure
Debt's cursed load, disease without a cure;
Thence made dependant — to the brighter mind
The harshest curse that can assail mankind.

* There are many money-lenders among the natives of
India, who readily supply any persons with what they may
want, but demand an exorbitant interest for the loan. If, at
the expiration of the time agreed on between the parties for
the reimbursement of the borrowed sum, the debtor is unable
to command it, the creditor frequently exercises all the rigours
of the law against him.

When once the Creditor's unhappy prey,
And threaten'd for the sum you cannot pay;
Grief's darkest agents constantly assail,
And paint the gloomy horrors of a gaol:
Tormented ev'ry hour by sordid Duns,
Grim Avarice's mercenary sons,
Thy breast with troublous pang incessant heaves,
As fost'ring peace the harass'd bosom leaves.
Whilst dread uncertainty dispels repose,
And superadds variety of woes;
Doubt, moody eld, the wounded mind invades,
And calls Despondence from her sombrest shades.
Whene'er a distant voice assails thine ear,
Instant thou deem'st some Creditor is near;
Or should a footstep follow thee behind,
The Bailiff's visage glows upon thy mind;
Whene'er a letter meets thy doubtful view,
Thine eyes the outward characters pursue;
Whilst dark suspicion chills thy trembling frame,
Lest it should bear the lawyer's hostile name.
Constant anxieties like these oppress,
Quicken thy grief, and make thee comfortless:—
At length arrives the hour, unwelcome fate,
That thou must pass the Prison's inward gate.

Here, robb'd of all that social life endears,
A constant prey to terrifying fears;
No friend, known seldom, to commiserate
Thy unforeseen and undeserving state;
Nought to beguile the dilatory day,
Which passes slow and sullenly away;
Left solely to the fretting goad of thought,
Unconscious where contentment may be sought;
Cast from the world to trace the Prison's gloom,
Whose horrors oft-times yield but to the tomb;
Within whose frowning walls but once immur'd,
Repute is lost, nor to be resecur'd.

When once bound fast by rough Confinement's chain,
Instantly tighten the strong cords of pain;
Upon the brow corroding Anguish lays
Her furrowing fingers, and her force essays;
To the unblushing cheeks forbids to flow
The healthful blood, in animating glow:
There Melancholy sits, in moody guise,
And to the heart her sharpest shaft applies:—
Sometimes she yields an anodyne to grief,
Yet *can* she wound as to defy relief:
Where she exerts her utmost pow'r to pain,
The best attempts at remedy are vain.

Depriv'd of Freedom, miserable thrall;
Encircled by the Prison's tow'ring wall:
Despis'd, abandon'd by the giddy few,
Who Folly's form in ev'ry dress pursue:
Alien from all, whose bosoms eager glow
To mock at grief, to spurn the child of wo:
Without one friend, one kind companion near,
To give the consolation of a tear:
Thy reputation foul'd by Scandal's tongue,
Whilst all her brood declare thee in the wrong.—
Once safe within the confines of a gaol,
To guard from scoffs, e'en Virtue's shield must fail
The croaking voice of Obloquy severe,
With painful censure, constant meets the ear.

In durance fix'd, what dire afflictions rise,
To shock the soul and moisten Pity's eyes!
Around are heard, distressing to declare,
The murd'rer's groans, the yellings of despair;
The voice of riot, mirth's distracted tone,
The shouts of rage, the penitential moan;
The yells of drunkenness, hoarse laughter's din,
With all the mighty turbulence of sin:—
Oaths, execrations, ev'ry rank excess
Has place in turn, and strangles happiness.

Strange 'tis that those, for some atrocious deed
Condemn'd to endless exile, or to bleed,
Should, all regardless of th' approaching wo,
Labour to 'stablish Mercy's Lord their foe;
Swallow the foul, prolific seeds of Vice,
And ever shut their souls from Paradise *.

Enough is here to chill the milder breast,
And cast a blighting mildew on it's rest;
To stop the strongest throes of selfish smart,
And cast Compassion's mantle o'er the heart.

Behold that guilty woman, madly wild,
Who gave to birth, then massacred her child!
Appalling horror chokes her lab'ring breath,
As dwells her mind upon approaching death;
Convuls'd she sits, the while her flashing eye
Is rais'd in supplication tow'rds the sky;

* I am fully persuaded, that frequently criminals, under
sentence of death, or transportation for life, commit all kinds
of excesses in the gaols where they may be confined: at least
this much I have on undoubted authority. I myself once saw
a man, condemned to death, in the cell where he was confined,
laughing, and often swearing at those who went to see or
condole with him.

But conscience pictures her inhuman deeds,
And gores her tortur'd bosom till it bleeds.

Here — where uncheck'd contentment ever fails —
Where meagre, skulking penury prevails :
Pinch'd hard by want, alas ! how many strive
To nourish life on what lean chance may give !
And urg'd, at length those hateful methods try,
By which they may, perchance, be doom'd to die.
Oft, just arisen from his couch of straw,
The wretched robber breaks his country's law ;
Steals the last penny from a fellow's purse,
And then, o'erjoy'd, rewards him with a curse*.

The gloomy gaol too often proves a school,
Where many a rogue is made of many a fool ;
Where those who 're only novices in crimes,
Learn Vice's darkest mysteries betimes ;

* It can scarcely, I should think, be doubted, that robbery
is frequently committed in prison : one felon, perhaps, plunders another, and exposes himself again to the severity of those
very laws which have already doomed him to punishment, and
that too whilst he is under the sentence of those laws. The
prison is, I fancy, but too often a dangerous school for every
kind of profligacy.

And, ere releas'd, deep skill'd in ev'ry art,
In ev'ry thrift that can pollute the heart.

Tho' chain'd and barr'd within the darken'd cell,
Where the rank walls exhale a fetid smell,
Where vermin breed secure and unannoy'd,
Left undisturb'd, nor e'er to be destroy'd:
The vicious felon, harden'd against fate,
Smiles at his low, dishonourable state;
Still points his soul to Vice's curst abode,
And, in the jaws of ruin, scoffs his God.

Tho' scarce asylum in the world below
Could mate the gaol in magnitude of wo;
Still often here will foul Excess be nigh,
Scatter her pests, and leave the wretch to sigh;
With rank disease unnerve his wasting form,
Now scarce a meal for the devouring worm.
Is harmony or concord ever found
Within the gaol's contaminating ground?
No,—'tis a place they shun, nor ever rest,
Unsullied, unassail'd, but with the blest:
Here Guilt constructs her dwelling-house; here dwell,
Beneath man's form, the agents oft of Hell.

Oh, thou for debt disastrously restrain'd
By prison walls, how must thy soul be pain'd
For here thou may'st explore the narrow cell,
Where Want repines and Horror loves to dwell:
Where, on the straw-made pallet stretch'd along,
The harden'd felon roars the blust'rous song;
Or with some other, occupied in play,
In Care's despight, games out the tardy day;
Robs his companion of his scanty store;
Goes to the next, and plunders as before.

Here the sad wretch, by poverty subdued,
Whose ruthless dagger drank a brother's blood;
Curses the awful hour that gave him breath,
Condemn'd to die a just, tho' dreadful death;
Watch'd night and day, with galling fetters bound,
And venting groans, stretch'd anguish'd on the ground:
Despair fast griping at his throbbing breast,
Gives horror birth and bars indulgent rest;
Tears at his heart-strings with ferocious fangs,
Whilst Fancy seems to point to where he hangs.

Now mark that wretched suff'rer, doom'd to die
For—urg'd by want—an act of forgery!
List to the tale, and as it meets thine ear,
Vouchsafe for once the sympathetic tear:

Trapp'd by Adversity—a wife rever'd,
With three-fond children, by that wife endear'd;—
His all exhausted, and his infants' cries
For Nature's indispensable supplies,
Urge him, in evil hour, for their support
To forge*; sad thrift! his last and worst resort.
His piteous tale thou hear'st, nor this alone,
Sad scenes of daily wo increase thine own.
Around stalks Wretchedness, in surly guise,
And, harshly stern, his morbid scourge applies:
Disease, too, oft-times leaves his hidden throne,
And on these care-worn sons flies vengeful down;
From his dark urn the dread contagion flings,
Lets Anguish loose, and sharpens Torment's stings:
Pain active glides o'er many a sickly frame,
Whilst base neglect supports the kindling flame.

Many poor wretches, in the dungeon pent,
Where noxious vapours rise, nor find a vent;
Where nought's receiv'd that wasting strength repairs,
Expos'd to damp, unwholesome, fetid airs;

---

* I really believe that many, of otherwise irreproachable
characters, have suffered for the crime of forgery; possibly
often fatally compelled to hazard their lives for the immediate
support of a famishing family.

Here languish out their melancholy days,
Unmourn'd, unhonour'd, subjects of dispraise.

The wretched debtor, worn by care, and old,
With vestments scarce to keep him from the cold;
Depriv'd of ev'ry comfort, ev'ry pleasure,
Bearing Grief's load beyond the common measure;
Wastes all his hours on weak, unsolid schemes
Of future joys, mere visionary dreams,
That for a moment yield a suasive balm,
Till Disappointment spoils the treach'rous calm;
On Hope's horizon casts a thick'ning shade,
When all her visions at the instant fade.

What more ignoble to the nicer mind,
Than in the gaol's recess to be confin'd!
Where the poor robber by distress led on,
To rape the mite which industry had won,
Counts ev'ry passing moment as it flies,
Fated to view but one more morn arise;
Dejected clasps his impious hands to Heav'n,
Owns his lot just, yet sighs to be forgiv'n*.

* Whether or not the above picture of the dreadful scenes
to be witnessed in a gaol be a correct one, can be best
answered by those who have been exposed to the unfortunate

Oft are there many like thyself immur'd —
Too sad misfortune! hard to be endur'd!
Who, with contracted brows and looks of gloom,
Trace, in despondent march, their dreary room;
Some slowly wasting to an early grave,
Where worldly woes no influence can have;
Where no severe vicissitudes are found —
Of ev'ry joy or hap the awful bound.

Ah! who shall tell what scenes thine eyes assail,
The genuine, dreadful horrors of a gaol!
Horrors that beggar all the Muse's might,
That skulk to felon cells and mock the light * ! —
E'en when releas'd, a galling slur adheres,
Nor can'st thou shun the churl's unmanly jeers:

necessity of abiding there. As for myself, although it was
never my misfortune to be imprisoned, I have frequently gone
over a gaol, and been eye-witness to scenes that I never should
have expected to meet with in so sad a place. I really believe
the gaol to be exempt from no kind of vice that is practised
among mankind.

* There is no doubt that many horrible circumstances have
place in a gaol, which are never heard of beyond it's confines.
That every prison is the same, nor one better conducted than
another, it would be certainly false to affirm; but that any
prison is altogether free from such horrors as have been
glanced at above, I can scarcely believe.

Thou'rt then the butt 'gainst which Spite wings her dart,
Long steep'd in gall, to vex the anguish'd heart;
Nor fails loud Scandal's tongue it's aid malign,
Prompt at a lie to gloze a foul design;
For in this hostile world we daily see
The imps of Fortune scoff at Misery.

When the dark porpoise, playing on the tide,
Receives the barb'd harpoon into his side;
Soon as the sanguine current dyes the flood,
His species crowd around and suck his blood,
Mangle the carcass, spoil the hold of breath,
And tear the wounded animal to death!
Thus oft does man,—self reigns supreme with all—
One stands exalted by another's fall;
He who is wounded by Misfortune's dart,
Has Slander's thousand daggers aim'd against his heart.

When from confinement's miseries releas'd,
Will ev'ry sad disquietude have ceas'd?
Despis'd by many, subject to disdain,
No solace offer'd to assuage thy pain:
Disgrace, remorseless canker-worm of Fame,
Brands thy fair brow and spots thine injur'd name.

Few have the noble candour to allow
That those whom hard Misfortune dooms to bow,
Deserve compassion. Oft, alas ! we hear
The rigid Cynic, judge but too severe,
Censure in rudest terms, when Pity's eyes
Should yield her tears, a moisture to her sighs.
But no ! too frequent when Affliction scowls,
And Fortune chang'd, a frightful monster, prowls;
Arm'd with severe anxieties to pain,
Whom Fate to worldly woes might pre-ordain : —
Many who soar aloft on eagle wing,
And sip the sweets success may chance to bring;
Revile the wretched, fancifully wise,
And call them Vice and Folly's progenies ;
Impute to Indiscretion all their woes,
Proclaim them Evil's champions, Virtue's foes. —
Thus, whilst their rugged hearts no kindness bear,
They spurn, with eyes of pride, the sons of Care;
Upon them cast the angry glance of Scorn,
And from their tongues thrust Slander's fest'ring thorn.
But should the tablets turn, and adverse Chance
Against these pamper'd May-flies hurl the lance,
How would they answer th' unexpected call ?
Vain in their rise, yet abject in their fall.

Oh, ill-starr'd Rational! for whom my song
It's humbly pensive strain would still prolong,
When thou'rt releas'd from fell Confinement's thrall,
Does joy go forth and welcome Freedom's call?
No! the foul macula of dark Disgrace
Throb at thy heart and mantle in thy face!
Tho' Innocence * may some kind solace bring,
Still will Contempt put forth it's active sting;
And mocking gibes jar hateful on thine ear,
Arouse Disgust, and wring the bitter tear:
Soon shall Despair thy vital functions freeze,
And Sorrow's cup be swallow'd to the lees.

Long look'd for patronage is now withheld,
And ev'ry hop'd for happiness dispell'd;
No place of trust can that poor youth assume,
Who once has known a Prison's cheerless gloom:
He's shunn'd by all, as if Contagion stalk'd
Close at his heels, and follow'd where he walk'd;
Denied Society's endearing sweets,
And, as a pest, revil'd by all he meets.

* Innocent as to any thing criminal, the debt supposed to be
incurred from causes already suggested.

Gloomy this picture, dark is ev'ry hue,
Yet will Experience often find it true ;
And quickly know, that in this distant land,
Where Britons all the Briton's friend should stand,
Chill Inhumanity bears mighty sway,
Whilst few are found but her commands obey.

Pause here—behold the melancholy man!
Scarce can the Muse his fierce emotions scan.
Heav'ns! When Affliction's blacken'd cup is drain'd,
And, by the draught, the heart to torture pain'd,
Who shall resist it's deleterious force,
Or of stern Torment strive t' arrest the course?—
Methinks I see the workings of Despair
Poison his brain, and riot vengeful there;
Whilst the grim fiend, with aspect foully drear,
Whispers forbade destruction in his ear;
Heaps up the loads of anguish on his breast,
Gripes firmly there, and bars pacific rest.

Ye vain, who glitter in the pride of state,
Who roll in wealth, or riot with the great,
Sink into Pleasure's enervating arms—
A siren mask'd, belied by borrow'd charms:—
And ye who never felt Affliction's thorn,
To humbler competence propitious born,

Mark the result of unrelaxing wo,
Almost too keen for man to undergo.

Behold the wretched youth, his spirit crush'd,
Each active sense in vacant torpor hush'd,
Yield himself up reluctant to his grief,
And from the pois'nous bottle seek relief;
Drink the unmeet potation, to allay
Those scorching fires which on his vitals prey;
Chase the kind cherub Hope, and in her room
Involve himself in Desperation's gloom.

That mind which late enthusiastic swell'd,
Where Genius flam'd too bright to be repell'd;
Now, by the weight of anguish overborne,
Sinks in Despair, from Hope's last anchor torn.

Behold the man, once nobly form'd to please,
A sluggard now, corrupted by disease;
Induc'd at last to try the potent bowl,
To chase the agony that wounds his soul!
Glass after glass he gulps successive down,
To fire his brain, offensive thought to drown:—
Observe him stare aloft with bursting eyes,
As to his cheeks the mantling currents rise;

Obscene with filth, his black and lolling tongue
Out of his mouth in idiot stupor hung;
Reason dispell'd, each faculty expir'd,
Which once was only known to be admir'd. ——
Oh, horror! horror! stern is thy controul,
How do thy goadings agonize the soul! ——
Subdued by Grief, by Fortitude forsook,
The fiends of Madness glare in ev'ry look;
His voice is rais'd in Bacchanalian cries,
And, unconcern'd of aught, he drinks and dies*.

Thus she, who bears upon her cheek the rose,
And on whose features modest beauty glows;
Once by the hardy libertine defil'd,
Each softer grace departs whence late it smil'd;
And the lost maiden, urg'd to foul desires,
Drinks Vice's fetid current and expires.

* I am firmly persuaded, from what has come under my own immediate observation, that many in India feel such a perfect unsolicitude about their existence, and merely too occasioned by their dislike to the country, that they would scarcely exert themselves to prolong it. The bottle is frequently resorted to, to beguile any time that may hang too heavy, and to give a flow of spirits where the mind has been long dull. Drinking certainly proves destructive to a vast number in this unfortunate country.

He who, till lately, challeng'd ev'ry grace,
The rays of Genius beaming from his face,
Now bloated lies, disgusting to the view,
Revil'd by many, mourn'd, alas! by few:
Not even Death hath pow'r to thaw the breast,
Where int'rest and self-love conjointly rest.

Is such the fate of him who quits his home,
O'er India's inauspicious wilds to roam?
Driv'n by unkindness to encounter Death,
And breathe, in Sin's embrace, his latest breath?
Truth boldly tells such horrors have been known,
But Pity slumber'd and denied her moan;
All such unnat'ral, undelighting themes,
Sunk quickly in Oblivion's deepest streams*.

Here may the dead have rest! Unhappy he,
Who for this land adventures on the sea!
The land where Hell-taught mysteries prevail,
Where all the more benignant virtues fail:

---

* I am sorry,—but truth compels me,—to say, that in however
calamitous a manner a person may meet his death in India, he
is consigned, generally speaking, unregretted to the grave; and
many there are who even rejoice at the circumstance.

Where Murder, issuing from the den of Night,
Walks undisguis'd abroad, and braves the light;
Where Superstition rolls her sightless eyes,
And opes her vast arcana to the skies;
Creates new gods, and, impiously blind,
Pours her stark venom o'er the menial mind;
Where at the altar oft the Priest has stood,
And stain'd the hallow'd pile with human blood;
Where oft the new-elected Rajah stands,
And dips in bubbling gore his impious hands;
Marks his swarth temples* with the sanguine dye,
Whilst shouts profane mount hateful to the sky;
Where the poor wretch, fanatically blind,
To the worst throes of agony resign'd,
Tears out his tongue; and, in Devotion's mood,
Smears the black idol with the trickling blood.

'Twas here of old, by human foot untrod,
Save the rare few devoted to their God,
Where the lone cave, in some dark wood conceal'd,
Saw horrid myst'ries practis'd unreveal'd;

* This is a custom amongst the Ghelote tribe. See Mau-
-rice's " Indian Antiquities ;" a book containing much valuable
information on Indian history.

Where, never pervious to the solar beam,
Bubbled the turbid, foul, infectious stream;
Where no indulgent breezes ever play'd,
Where never beast could seek refreshing shade;
Where clotted gore of human victims slain,
Crimson'd the walls, and dyed the gloomy plain : —
Here, — save the priest, with trembling step and slow,
Affrighted paleness on his sunken brow,
Who went to celebrate, with fearful heed,
Those rites unto his monstrous God decreed, —
No guilty mortal ever dar'd to tread,
Lest ruin should be hurl'd upon his head.

Here, 'mid the dismal terrors of the night,
When from her sombre cell stalk'd forth Affright,
The weak Hindoo, by priesthood wiles deceiv'd —
Nought of the Bramin's doctrines disbeliev'd, —
Stirr'd up his soul's enthusiastic fire,
And, push'd by phrensy, dar'd to God aspire;
By cruel penance mortified his frame,
And to immortal honours laid a claim.

How oft th' infatuated Indian dies,
To seek a safe asylum 'mid the skies !
Horrid the tortures which he undergoes,
To yield his soul it's last and best repose.

'One while with ordure * he besmears his frame,
And gives it fearless to the kindling flame; ·
Stands unappall'd, and courts the crackling fires,
Till, all his carcass roasted, he expires.
Oft the proud Devotee himself denies
Food for support, and, famish'd, calmly dies:
Sometimes his enervated body throws
In some deep hollow, fill'd with gelid snows† ;
Or seeks the Ganges' stream, and prays the while,
Till eaten by the hungry crocodile.
Frequent he cuts his throat in Reason's spite,
Where, sacred chance, two confluent streams unite;
Thinking, when God the action shall descry,
He'll haste his soul to seek a brighter sky.

Oh thou, in climates less ungenial rear'd,
Where HE of Heav'n is more sublimely fear'd,
Pause upon this!!——Here vainly may'st thou mourn
Days long elaps'd, nor fated to return,

* Cow dung is invariably used for such purposes. All those
particular modes of destruction noticed above, were practised,
and I believe are still, in this country, as self-sacrifices to their
sanguinary deities.

† It is scarcely needful to say, that snows are not a little
abundant in the more northern parts of Asia.

When Innocence unconscious swell'd thy breast,
Lay on thy pillow, and prolong'd thy rest.—
Fond Mem'ry cease, nor longer thus impart
Such subtle torment to the wounded heart.

Again 'tis meet the harass'd mind explore
A joyless state, where peace shall be no more.

Hapless advent'rer, in these regions wild !
Sport of mischance, and Grief's adopted child !
Sunder'd from all the heart considers dear,
And thrown a solitary wand'rer here ;
Should'st thou but cast thine ardent gaze around,
In search of Friendship, 'tis not to be found ;
For, like the Sage's visionary stone *,
We *find* it not, we *hear* of it alone.

None can be notic'd here without his fee,
Gold's the sole passport to society ;
Nor education, talent, aught avail,
When pompous rank and better riches fail.
No beauteous fair one here a glance can deign,
Except on those who wear the smiles of gain,

* The Philosopher's stone.

Or such as bear a high, tho' empty *name ;*
Shallow of heart, of mind the very same.
Those women, too, who sneer at humble worth,
Can often boast nor family, nor birth ;
Mere paltry bargains, refuse of the mart,
Who get new trimm'd, then try to rape a heart ;
And, when their native Isle unfriendly proves,
Quit their dull homes for Ind's *Idalian* groves;
Here gull old dotards with imperfect charms,
Jingle their cash, then take them to their arms ;
Leer them to love, then gain the name of wife,
And in their sides remain a thorn for life.
Now cover'd by the matrimonial shield,
Abroad they range on Inclination's field,
Wink at each well-dress'd puppy that they meet,
And strive to bring him kneeling at their feet :
Which done, the fopling soon becomes a guest,
And the poor husband dwindles to a *beast* *.

* It can scarcely be necessary to say, that this does not extend to all the women in India. Many very amiable characters are to be met with, no doubt; but, taken in the gross, they are certainly not angels.

END OF THE FOURTH PART.

THE CADET.

Part the Fifth.

Now would the melancholy Muse explore
The *mighty blessings* of this *blissful* shore!!

Whene'er kind Heav'n it's wonted boon denies,
And moist'ning clouds forsake the parching skies,

(Nor seldom this,) gaunt Famine spoils the land,
And thousands perish 'neath her griping hand;
A drought prevails, starvation presses on,
And Horror's legions growl o'er sire and son;
Fear stalks at large, and, join'd by wild Affright,
Subdues each heart, and triumphs in it's might:
The grinning King of Terrors gluts his fill,
Whilst gory havoc marks his furious will:
Ruin extends o'er ev'ry fertile plain,
And pray'r and penance both perform'd in vain:
The famish'd cattle, sheep and oxen, die,
Rot on the ground, and there corrupted lie:
Groans, dying shrieks, convulsive murmurs rise,
And on the wings of Horror mount the skies:
Gigantic Mis'ry in it's direst dress,
Triumphs o'er all whom Fortune chanc'd to bless;
Strangles Contentment's lamb, the dove of Peace,
And bids the bosom's placid throbbings cease:
Rank putrefaction fills the fetid air —
The carrion ravens scent their distant fare,
And, hoarsely croaking, perch upon the spoil,
Scatt'ring the mangled fragments o'er the soil.

As soon as Death has drunk the vital flood,
These clam'rous spoilers glut their carrion food;

Tear out the eyes *, and leave th' unsightly clay
A frightful spectacle to work dismay.
The stubborn land looks gashly with it's load,
Where Desolation holds his curs'd abode;
Corruption ev'ry where manures the ground,
And noxious, useless herbage springs around;
At large Contagion stalks with active stride,
Casting her baleful ruin far and wide;
With rotting fingers gripes the cherub Health,
And feeds on Life's invaluable wealth.

How vast the shock that thousands undergo!
A horrid, but irremeable wo!
Depriv'd of sustenance, unnerv'd they lie
On the rank earth, and, unassisted, die,
Whilst the slim corpse remains where, ere life fled,
The hapless victim fix'd his latest bed.

* The crows and ravens generally commence on a carcass
by picking out the eyes. The Parsee cast of people, who
after death expose the bodies of their relatives to these car-
nivorous birds, always visit the defunct a short time after he
has been thus exposed, to see which eye is plucked out: if the
right, they expect their souls will visit Paradise: if the left,
their place of purgatory. If both are gone, the case, of course,
remains doubtful.

Deform'd and mangled by the birds of prey,.
Expos'd it lies to Sol's malignant ray;
Not destin'd e'en to load the pious bier,
No tender friend to drop a parting tear :—
The sterile land denies the friendly pyre,
And not one carcass feeds the fun'ral fire.

Such are not all the horrors which arise
From Famine's den,—not half her miseries !
The worst misfortunes witness'd upon earth
Obey her call, and instant spring to birth:
ATE, fell Evil's parent, owns her pow'r,
And Hell's worst torments at her footstool cow'r.

Picture the monster, — from Tartarean lakes, —
Her squalid brows o'erhung with hissing snakes ;
Her sunken jaws with fangs of rusty steel,
Arm'd on each side, like spokes of waggon wheel;
Her sallow cheeks, with bones that seem to rise,
To form a hollow for her gleaming eyes;
Her nostrils open wide, in vengeful mood,
Discharge black smoke and gouts of clotted blood:
Her brows, deep furrow'd, tortur'd to a scowl,
Shap'd like the forehead of a monstrous owl ;
Her ears hang pendant, like uncurried hides,
And part conceal her lank and bony sides:

As clearest crystal balls, of mighty size,
Glare, gashly luminous, her Gorgon eyes;
Her carrion lips, with maggots pregnant, seem
Like muddy banks, min'd under by the stream;
Her breasts resemble bladders void of wind,
O'ersoil'd with filth, deform'd with sores unkind :
Her nether parts, disgusting to behold,
Roll vast along, in many a length'ning fold ;
A monstrous sight — whilst eager round her waist.
Voracious Harpies clamour for their feast:
Alternate each within her arms she hugs,
And feeds the scraggy monsters from her dugs ;
Then sets them on to work her fell behest,
Whilst gasping Horror issues from her breast :
Seizes on all, and Famine at his heels
Speeds on, and in her own corruption reels *.

* This may very possibly be censured, by those who chance
to read it, as a most disgusting prosopopœia. I will not
attempt to deny it; but thus much I can venture to advance,
that the above picture cannot create one hundredth part as
much disgust in the reader, as a sight of the horrible effects of
famine would in the beholder. India is frequently the theatre
on which famine appears in it's most shocking character. My
sole object, in the above sketch, was to impress upon the mind
somewhat of the feelings which a view of the miseries of
famine would naturally excite. Although a personification of

Such fancy Famine, here so often known,
Sent from the deadly shores of Acheron ;
From whose embitter'd streams, when she ascends,
Man prostrate falls, and shock'd Creation bends ;
Nature puts on the sombre stole of gloom,
And seems to sorrow o'er her offspring's tomb.
Thousands are forc'd to leave their lands of birth,
Pursued by want to seek some stranger earth :
There, cruel Fortune ! often doom'd to live
Upon the mite stint Charity may give ;
No house to shield their enervated forms
From nightly dews, from cold and whistling storms ;

this great earthly calamity might have been dispensed with,
from the poem into which it is introduced admitting nothing
of fable, still, as it derogates in nowise from the dignity of
truth ; but, according to my probably circumscribed judgment, serves, on the contrary, to paint it in more glowing
colours, it may not be altogether found irrelevant to the
subject. Should it, after all, offend, the reader may pass it
over as a few worthless lines, and proceed to what may less
disgust him. I must still offer him this excuse on my own
behalf : — Having been myself in some measure an eye-witness
to the horrible effects of famine in India, where whole coun-
tries are sometimes almost depopulated ; upon entering on the
subject, the figure of famine presented itself so forcibly to my
imagination, that I could not rest satisfied until I had taken
the picture.

Expos'd, unshelter'd, on the swampy ground,
Where baleful damps fall drearily around;
Nor aught to ward them from the chilly air
But partial rags, their bodies almost bare:—
Wives, husbands, infants, in one common bed,
Where rugged stones support each weary head.

Frequent, when radiant Morn illumes the East,
Warning the world that Night's dull hours have ceast,
Some half-starv'd mother quits her rocky bed,
Looks at her side, and finds her infant dead;
Shock'd at the sight, uplifts her streaming eyes,
Clasps her weak hands to Heaven, groans and dies*.

List to that mourner, wailing o'er her child,
With hair erect and eyes all haggard wild!
Oh, how the piercing accents wound the ear,
Draw forth the sigh, and wring the gath'ring tear!

* During a late partial famine in this country, in the province of Guzzerat, people might frequently be seen dying and
dead in the roads; and even in Bombay, where some thousands had taken refuge, scenes of a similar nature were sometimes witnessed, before places could be erected to receive the
unfortunate sufferers. Funeral fires were continually blazing
on the beach for some weeks together.

" Wherefore, sweet baby, that unconscious smile,
" Unknowing what thy parent feels the while?
" Had thy untuneful tongue but learn'd to speak,
" No smile would now be dimpling on thy cheek;
" But the dark frown of horrible Despair
" Had mark'd thy brow, and left it's furrow there.

" Those milky streams which late thy wants supplied,
" Are all absorb'd, their fost'ring fountains dried;
" Nothing remains to answer hunger's call,
" For sateless Want has long exhausted all.
" All-righteous Providence! severely just,
" Who humblest proudest nations to the dust,
" A Mother's lowly deprecation hear,
" Avert her wo, nor wing the shaft of Fear—
" 'Tis past — I feel the angry hand of Heav'n!
" To dust this wretched frame must soon be giv'n!
" Who then, poor Baby, shall thy life sustain,
" Or from thy bosom pluck the barb of Pain?
" None will be found—'twere better cease to live,
" Than bear the strokes Calamity may give!—
" Yes, 'tis resolv'd — be Death thy present doom,
" He shall exempt thee now from woes to come."

Here, raising high her voice, in accent wild,
And gazing furious o'er her slumb'ring child—

" Yes — thou'rt mine own, 'twas I that gave thee birth,
" Groan'd for thy sake, and priz'd thine infant worth;
" I've fed thee, nurs'd thee with unceasing care;
" For what? To give thee victim to Despair?
" Sweet sleeping Innocent! Celestial Pow'rs!
" Wing the pure soul to Bliss's hallow'd bow'rs!
" 'Tis hunger calls, her voice must be obey'd —
" Come from my bosom forth, remorseless blade,
" Drink the young stream."—With that, in frenzied mood,
She bathes the dagger in her infant's blood.

Happy the child who tastes unconscious Death,
Ere Famine breathes her pestilential breath;
Who thus, in happiest days, avoids the strife,
Which ever marks this sublunary life;
Seeking a home where no fierce sorrows throng,
Where angel spirits swell th' eternal song:—
How blest above all those pre-doom'd to live
On the stint morsel Chance may sometimes give!

Ill fated baby! born in Famine's reign,
Destin'd to drink the broadest cup of pain!
Want and Distress receive thee from the womb,
Whilst weeping Pity trembles at thy doom.
Thy Parents, giv'n Affliction's force to feel,
Crush'd by the weight of Fortune's adverse wheel,

Hail thy sad birth with lamentable cries,
And give their first caress with bodeful sighs.

How oft shall Nature sicken to behold —
To feed the Sire — the starving infant sold:
Sold to be pinch'd by Slav'ry's galling chain,
And giv'n to weep for Liberty in vain;
Sold by a Father, — dead to tend'rer grief, —
From Hunger's gripe to gain a short relief.

Ye who, at ease, ne'er tempted to explore
The mighty woes which crowd a torrid shore,
Well may ye start, but Truth confronts ye here,
Nor can her aspect well be more severe;
She wakes the brood of Anguish in the heart,
And the prob'd bosom pants beneath the smart.

Oft when stern Famine, with insatiate ire,
Rages abroad, like Hell's sulphureous fire;
Some hapless mother, desperately wild,
Sells*, for a scanty meal, her darling child;

* It is a circumstance by no means uncommon, during the
prevalence of famine, to see mothers sell their children for a
meal of rice.

Devours the morsel with voracious speed,
And curses then the unparental deed !
Repentant now the anguish'd Mother mourns,
Whilst all her fondness for her babe returns ;
Wanders forlorn, from home and country cast,
And, marr'd of ev'ry comfort, starves at last.
So the poor redbreast, when chill Winter reigns,
Numb'd by the cold, flees hasty from the plains ;
From spray to spray in search of food he flies,
But, disappointed, droops his wings and dies.

Ye who can pluck from Plenty's blooming tree,
To feed th' impure desires of Luxury ;
Who take the choicest dainties from her board,
To load the pampering, voluptuous board ;
Pause a brief while on their afflicting doom,
Whom Want relentless hastens to the tomb :
Then spurn the temper'd dish, and call to mind,
How God can punish where he feels inclin'd.
Reflect on those whom adverse Fortune brings
Beneath lank Scarcity's outspreading wings ;
Forc'd oft to leave their offspring at the door,
Where Av'rice rests and growls upon the poor :
Or worse — to give their infant as a slave,
To keep the helpless suff'rer from the grave ;

Leave the dear baby with a boding sigh,
Contend themselves with want, and, famish'd, die.

Now the poor orphan, rear'd to constant toil,
Scarce ever finds a respite from turmoil;
Mourns the malignant hour that gave him birth,
An unbefriended outcast upon earth;
Scorn'd as a drudge, neglected and despis'd,
No hope of comfort ever realiz'd :—
Each hour assumes the same unvarying round
Of stubborn labour; never to be found
A soothing lenitive, a grateful balm,
To turn his soul's high workings into calm—
Yet still a greater curse is sometimes felt
Than that, by Destiny, to Slav'ry dealt.

Alas! how dreadful is it to behold
The frequent pow'r of mercenary gold!
That base polluter of the brightest mind!
That bane, but fancied blessing to mankind!
Sometimes the Mother, by rough Want opprest,
Tears the young female infant from her breast;
And gives it for some despicable price,
To be train'd up within the fane of Vice.
Sold to some Debauchee, whose highest joy
Consists, with good, to mingle ill's alloy;

The thoughtless child is rear'd in Whoredom's arms,
And taught to prize alone her baneful charms;
Train'd 'mid the frantic orgies of excess,
Array'd in Lust's too fascinating dress;
Instructed in venereal wiles, and rear'd
In all those vices most by Virtue fear'd;
Bred to inthrall, to rouse impure desire,
To fan Salacity's intemp'rate fire:—
Thus, ere the fleeting days of childhood close,
The vast arcana of Love's shrine she knows*.
As soon as shall the plastic hand of Time
Give her pubescence, then the heinous crime
Of fell seduction blots her fairest day,
And plucks indignant Virtue's staff away.

* This is certainly a most horrible truth; but is, nevertheless, often known in India. The mother of a female infant
very frequently, when oppressed by want, sells her child, to be
prostituted by some wealthy native. If the poor unfortunate
child be very young, it is trained up to practise every seductive art that can arouse the more lascivious passions: and even
in the days of infancy,—at ten or eleven years old,—robbed
of virginity, and kept for the brutal enjoyment of some old and
diseased libertine. Europeans in India, I am sorry to say,
often purchase these miserable infants from the same de-
testable motives; and frequently, after seducing them and
depriving them of the rights of their cast, leave them to a
miserable fate.

Awhile she blooms in Beauty's transient hour;
Blooms but to mourn it's transitory pow'r!

How drear the life the hapless victim leads,
For whom benign Compassion never pleads !
Forc'd Freedom's dearest rights to sacrifice,
And owe subsistence to the hire of Vice;
Watch'd by fierce Jealousy's suspicious eye,
And oft oblig'd to frame the ready lie;
To feign the willing dalliance of love,
A nerveless dotard's beastly smile to move;
Of Infidelity oft-times accus'd,
And for suspected errors misabus'd :—
She leads a life of ev'ry joy divest,
And bears the load of anguish on her breast;
Denied those social joys to others known,
Robb'd of her peace, existence scarce her own :—
In sad uncertainty her days expire,
Priz'd but to stop the cravings of desire;
Dependant for support on wild caprice,
Nor conscious e'en when that support may cease :—
For, should the man who stole her virgin gem,
And pluck'd the bud of Virtue from it's stem*,

* Here is confessedly a pleonasm; but I trust it does not injure or disgrace the sense.

Pall'd by enjoyment, drive her from his gate,
And yield her friendless to the storms of fate;
Where may she wander then? Revil'd by all,
To answer Hunger's unrelenting call,
Necessity with cruel Want conspires,
To make her grasp at Prostitution's hires.
For some small mite to lust she yields her charms,
And clasps obscene disease within her arms;
Whilst the contagion to her frame adheres,
Robs her at last of life, and dries Affliction's tears.

Woes such as these from Famine oft arise,
Sent by the mighty Regent of the skies!
Ye heav'nly Pow'rs! to birth what horrors spring,
When the huge Monster spreads her harpy wing!
Here known so frequent! — ev'ry day we find
Some woful trace which she has left behind.

India! deluding name! where are those stores
Which Rumour tells o'erload thy boundless shores?
Where, too, those favour'd nations, born to bliss,
Who never stoop the rod of Care to kiss? —
Delusion all! — In India's deserts wild
Famine has oft'ner frown'd than Plenty smil'd * !

* I have been given to understand, and cannot but yield it
every credit, that scarcely a year passes but some slight effects
of famine are felt on the Asian continent.

Who, born in Liberty's prolific Isle,
Where Nature's rudest sons may dare to smile*;
Where murder seldom durst approach the light,
But hides her in her den of blackest night;—
Who, nurtur'd 'mid Britannia's verdant plains,
Where rural comfort oft so calmly reigns,
Could live on Ind's ungratifying waste,
And of Contentment's crystal goblet taste?

Let Pity's dewy eye be cast around
On the vast track of Oriental ground;
Let it explore the miserable cell,
Where mad Devotion's maniac vot'ries dwell;
There let it mark the fanatic commence,
To purge his tainted soul from foul offence —
Tied by the feet, aloft in air he swings,
And, lash'd the while, to God profanely sings;
For three long hours his knotted heels† in air,
He clasps his hands and breathes incessant pray'r;

* In England, the peasants,—there considered the rudest
sons of Nature,—are just as free to think and act as are
the highest personages: it certainly is not thus in every
country.

† This is a penance adopted by the Fakeer tribe, swinging
for a certain number of hours every day by the heels; which
many of them do until deprived of power to assist themselves.

The while his downward head, by blood surcharg'd,
Aches with it's weight, prodigiously enlarg'd : —
Thus he remains, till, all sensation flown,
By some companion he's at last let down.

Who, born where Freedom spreads her heav'nly ray,
And lights the track of life's bewild'ring way,
Would seek a home on India's sun-parch'd ground,
Where social pleasures never shall be found ;
Where despicable Tyranny presides ;
Where Guilt with all her thousand imps abides ;
Where Superstition rears her speckled crest,
In monster robes magnificently drest ;
Hail'd as a goddess, worshipp'd as divine,
Tho' human gore has oft besmear'd her shrine ?

What are the penances the hag prescribes
To her unnumber'd, unenlighten'd tribes ?
Some shall be noted, tho' no pen could draw
All the dark rites begotten from her law.

First mark the recent widow, madly brave,
Triumphant clamour for an early grave ;
Demand to seek her last long earthly home,
And with her spouse partake the dreary tomb ;

In youth's best prime her worldly joys give o'er,
To gain those realms where Death can frown no more.
Behold her undisturb'd, with accent mild,
Bestow a hasty blessing on her child ;
Give the poor babe a mother's last embrace,
And print the parting kiss upon it's face ;
Consign the infant to some kindred friend,
And, undepress'd, prepare to meet her end !

Beguil'd unfortunate ! had truth reveal'd
What Superstition has from thee conceal'd,
Thou would'st have known, that God, in ev'ry clime,
Frowns on self-murder, reprobates the crime !
But, train'd in *false* Devotion's bloody fane,
Where 'tis conceiv'd a crime to be humane ;
Whose tenets teach that Cruelty should rest,
Nor e'er be absent from the human breast ;
Each harden'd vot'ry in Devotion's mood,
Spurns at Compassion, smiles on human blood.

How doubly blest is he, compar'd with these
Who basely spurn at Heav'n's sublime decrees ---
Born where Religion's brightest glories shine,
Irradiated by a hand divine ; ---
Who, onward led by truth's unerring light,
Can see what distance lies 'twixt wrong and right !

Mark the huge pile, high tow'ring 'mid the air,
Erected quaint, design'd with cautious care ;
Crown'd with huge beams of ample weight and size,
To crush the victim as the flames arise ;
With sapless straw at intervals o'erspread,
By which the blaze may be the better fed,
Strew'd o'er with unguents, to assist the fire,
And sooner wrap in flame the greedy pyre.

Four spiral poles the ligneous mass enclose,
Of equal size and strength precisely chose ;
Fix'd in the ground, in oblong form they stand,
Six feet of length the light foundation's plann'd ;
Distant three feet the upright props appear,
Within which space the fabric's bulk they rear ;
Dry crumbling wood is lightly pil'd on high,
While smoking incense blazes to the sky.
The destin'd victim standing by serene,
Unmov'd regards the agonizing scene ;
Absorb'd in holy thought directs her eyes,
In fix'd expression, to th' o'er-arching skies ;
Wafts forth some pious pray'r with ev'ry breath,
And seems unconscious of approaching death :
Sometimes a momentary glance she lends
To those around she ranks among her friends ;

Gives them her benediction, and the while
Bestows on all a melancholy smile.

Now she prepares, with looks of fix'd intent,
For that dread act on which her soul is bent,
Performs whate'er her ritual prescribes,
And gives her blessing to th' assembled tribes.
The last ablution o'er, her friends the while
Around her thronging, lead her to the pile;
To each some small donation she presents,
Till she exhausts her various ornaments;
Save sole the marriage knot, first giv'n to deck,
At Hymen's hallow'd shrine, her olive neck,
And one rude band, which binds the naked arm,
And holds some secret, efficacious charm.

Now with her palms uprais'd in silent pray'r,
Invoking SEEVA's tutelary care,
She sits her down beside the putrid dead,
And on her lap displays the lifeless head;
Upon the corpse bestows a last embrace,
Then draws the linen mantle o'er her face.
Her feet now firmly plac'd upon the pyre,
She takes a brand and gives the fabric fire;

The crafty Bramin* standing nigh the while,
In various places lights the kindling pile:
Instant the flames in ruddy volumes rise,
And urge the smoke impetuous to the skies;
Sends forth the crowded mob discordant screams,
Till the poor suff'rer's crush'd beneath the beams,
Which pond'rous fall, suspended o'er her head,
And quick o'erwhelm the living with the dead.
Mark what loud yells distend each savage throat!
Hear mad infatuation's horrid note!
Drunk with unholy joy, the mob on high
Send their hoarse shouts and drown the suff'rer's cry!

How dire the customs of this torrid clime!
They shock the soul, and mar the pow'rs of rhyme!
Here Superstition holds unquestion'd reign,
Her sceptre's sway'd o'er ev'ry Indian plain;
And sanguine Cru'lty, of coëval birth,
Hies at her beck, to fright this ruder earth.

When angry Heav'n denies it's wonted rain,
And steril Desolation blasts the plain;

* The officiating Bramin always applies a torch to the pile:
on such occasions a number of Bramins generally assemble.

When the vast tank, which all his wants supplied,
By Sol's malignant orb is drank and dried;
The timid Indian, struck with instant fear,
Deems some malignant agent to be near:
When the parch'd land denies the foodful rice,
He offers up averting sacrifice:
Famine he views, thro' Fancy's plastic eye,
A horrid monster of the darkest dye;
And to avert it's advent, bows him down
At CALLEE's altar, trembling at her frown.
His curdling blood with difficulty flows,
At thought of past and dread of future woes;
He deems no off'ring at a price too great,
To gain the god to stop the hand of Fate.
The wily Priest who CALLEE's will explains,
Ofttimes a bloody sacrifice ordains;
Alternately the child, and dearer wife,
Bleed at the altar 'neath the holy knife;
Whilst the poor suppliant — thus the rite decrees —
Sprinkles the bubbling gore upon his knees;
Smears the black Idol's visage, grim and foul,
And breathes the pious feelings of his soul.

When, homeward wending tow'rds his humble shed,
He thinks upon his wife or infant dead;

The sigh of lighten'd sorrow heaves his breast,
As Fancy paints those martyrs with the blest.

Now mark the miserable victim bound,
And to his shoulders buried in the ground;
Expos'd to the fierce Sun's intensest ray,
Which drains life's moisture by degrees away.
The cold damp earth benumbs his stiffen'd form,
Which, ere expires existence, feeds the worm;
Left without food, and raging with his pain,
He bites the stubborn ground, but bites in vain!
At length expended, one last effort tries,
Till, all his strength decay'd, unnerv'd he dies*!

Now let the moisten'd eye of Pity see
The torments of Oppression's fierce decree;
Where, for some hasty, unimportant deed,
The undeserving victim's doom'd to bleed;
Or worse, to bear impalement's agony,
Transfix'd and writhing, impotent to flee;

* This is a method that was at one time very much adopted
in India: it is now less prevalent: but among the Chinese, I
am told, it is still often resorted to by way of capital punishment.

Left to the scorching rigours of the day,
Life ebbing on, yet tardy in decay;
None to condole, by ev'ry tongue revil'd,
And rank'd as Infamy's atrocious child;
The groans call'd forth by cruel torture drown'd,
By clamours that from ev'ry side resound :—
With each strong struggle all the mob rejoice,
Scream their applause, and check Compassion's voice;
Curse the poor wretch, invoke th' infernal Pow'rs
To hurl his soul to YAMEN's penal bow'rs.
As life at length forsakes enshrouding clay,
And frees the soul to seek a brighter day;
Spurn'd is the corse, denied the kindly grave,
Nor e'en one friend the sad remains to save;
But left to scorch beneath meridian flame,
A feast for crows, for rav'nous kites the same;
Whilst unconsum'd, the bleach'd and crumbling bones
Lie careless scatter'd 'mid disjointed stones;
On which, as the lone trav'ller casts his eye,
He bans the hapless culprit's memory *.

---

* The punishments in India are sometimes excessively bar-
barous. I have never myself been eye-witness to the punishment of empalement, but am acquainted with those who have:
and, to give some idea in how disgusting a manner criminals

Are such the nations amongst whom to dwell,
So many bid their homes a last farewell?
Is this the people Rumour draws so mild?
Is this where genius primitively smil'd?
Yes! thus we're told:—the task indeed were great,
Each barb'rous orient practice to relate;
Beyond my inefficient pow'rs to draw
The foul corruptions of the Eastern law:
But, ere I close the melancholy song,
Terrors must still the gloomy strain prolong.

The week Hindoo, by priesthood crafts misled,
Expects his wife will follow when he's dead;
And thinks, with all his equipage, that she
In the next world will bear him company.
From mad ideas such as these arise
Spontaneous deaths, the fun'ral sacrifice;
Where oft the widow, with her female train,
Rears the dry pile upon the neighb'ring plain,
And, by her slaves attended, mounts the pyre,
Seizes a torch, and perishes by fire!

are sometimes treated in this country, I once saw, whilst on a
journey, five bodies hanging in the middle of the public road,
in a state of putrescence.

When some superior is by Death convey'd
To those vast realms to which no bounds are laid,
Victims unnumber'd feel the holy knife,
In hopes to serve him in a happier life*.

Fir'd with the mighty thought of bliss to come,
The frantic Indian often seeks the tomb;
With the keen lash of penance scars his frame,
And undergoes beyond what tongue can name;
Exults in torture, deeming soon to gain
A lasting home, beyond the reach of pain.
Thinking, when life's precarious spark shall fly,
To find a rest beyond this nether sky;
He binds himself by vows of horrid note,
To Superstition all his soul devote;—
Whole days escape, but still no food he tastes,
Till to a slim anatomy he wastes:
Then, to prolong his melancholy days,
Takes the scant rice, and eats it while he prays.
Sometimes in dreary solitude he 'll roam,
Forth wand'ring naked, just as from the womb:

* When any great personage dies, a Rajah for instance, a
great many of his slaves and dependants voluntarily sacrifice
themselves to his manes, in the hope of following and serving
him in the next world.

Onward he rambles, patient as a saint,
His silent tongue ne'er stirring in complaint;
He bears of heat and cold each dreadful change,
Nor 'mid the pelting storm forbears to range;
He fixes on the solar beam his eye,
Till by it's heat the visual orb is dry;
Or holds his arms erect for many a day,
Till flesh and sinews shrink at once away:—
Sometimes the rusty hook his members tear,
And, swung aloft, he wriggles in the air;
Still no complaint is heard, no inward groan,
Nor can the fiercest pain extract a moan;
Calmly and undisturb'd he undergoes
The most acute, inexplicable woes;
Bears all resign'd, in hopes, at life's last date,
To be rewarded from the hand of Fate *.

Here let us briefly mark the rites profane,
Oft practis'd in MEHADEO's filthy fane;
Where Vice her bestial† emblem wide displays,
And, 'neath Devotion's cloak, hides Virtue's rays.

* It is scarcely possible to imagine the severity with which
the Fakeer tribe torture themselves, in hopes of gaining an
habitation among the blessed in another world.
† The phallus is displayed upon the altars of this deity.

The crafty Priesthood who attend the god,
Forge the foul rituals of his curs'd abode;
Within his gloomy walls keep Lust confin'd,
And live a degradation to mankind.

Here female beauty, still in infant bloom,
Finds for a length of days a living tomb; —
Virgins are stol'n, and *nominally* giv'n
A stainless off'ring to indulgent Heav'n;
But, torn for ever from their parents' arms,
The priests despoil and riot in their charms.
Those tender maids — the curs'd irrev'rence note —
Are to the temple's impious god devote:
Whilst the foul ministers, profanely wise,
Gull their weak minds with truth-beseeming lies;
Cast o'er their senses Superstition's veil,
And teach them Vice, in Virtue's garb, to hail.

Be now MEHADEO's* inmost fane explor'd,
And how the monstrous god is there ador'd.

First are those infants from their parents ta'en,
And early train'd to ev'ry art profane;

* Mehadeo is the same with Seeva.

Instructed how to tantalize delight,
By charms expos'd t' attract the eager sight ;
Taught from their tend'rest days to rouse desire,
And fan unrighteous Love's intemp'rate fire : —
Oft, ere mature, the Bramins take their prey,
And pluck the prop of Innocence away.
Here are they taught the wanton eye to roll,
And fan the fire that kindles in the soul ;
T' invite unchaste indulgence by their smiles,
And court the gaze by fascinating wiles ;
To mould their airy bodies to the dance,
And brew the poison of Concupiscence : —
Here do licentious passions all unite
To crush Religion's fundamental rite ;
Whilst Prostitution, in these rank abodes,
Sits thron'd upon the altars of the gods *.

* Religion is but too often made use of as a cloak to cover
the most heinous enormities. In Mehadeo's temple are confined a number of those wretched women, who were first
devoted to the idol, then seduced by the priests. Their principal occupation is singing and dancing in the temple ; and, if
the writings of very credible authors may be relied on, they
frequently receive the wages of prostitution from strangers,
and devote the money, thus impiously and blasphemously
raised, to defray the expenses of the temple, consecrated to

Behold that victim, dragg'd to meet his doom,
Condemn'd to starve amid the Dungeon's gloom:
The Dungeon! Worse—it's horrors well may vie
With such as in Tartarean caverns lie.
Upright he stands, scarce room to turn is found,
Whilst circumambient walls enclose him round:—
Left here, of ev'ry nourishment denied,
And dies at last as thousands else have died *.

On some lone spot whence vegetation flies,
Where fiercest rage the fires of eastern skies;
Where the lone trav'ller seldom dares to tread,
The wretched culprit's doom'd to rest his head;
For some minute offence condemn'd to die,
Where ne'er may pierce the glance of mortal eye.
He stands encircled by the stubborn fence;
Sad Fate! his last terrestrial residence.
Depriv'd of sustenance, of light and air,
O'erburthen'd by the workings of Despair;

their most powerful deity, and to obtain for the Bramins in
secret the more luxurious enjoyments of life.
   * It is a custom in this country, sometimes to destroy
criminals by building round them, covering the structure in at
the top, and leaving the unfortunate sufferers there to perish.

Condemn'd to pass, by eager hunger prest,
The bound of life, and seek a doubtful* rest :
Anguish'd he groans his remnant hours away,
Pierc'd by the pricking arrows of dismay :
In thought, Death's voice continual strikes his ear,
And down his cheek fast falls the scalding tear :
At last the fiery fang of fever warms
His throbbing breast, and all his strength disarms ;
He sobs in rueful bitterness of grief,
And seeks in vain to yield his mind relief ;
Weary and faint, at length the suff'rer falls,
His meagre frame supported by the walls.

Exhausted now the victim faintly sighs,
As mocks the light his oft imploring eyes ;
Darkness intense the drear abode pervades,
Black as the dens where rest the outcast shades.
Absorb'd in bitter agony of soul,
His madden'd brain spurns Reason's calm controul ;
To force the walls, his utmost efforts foil'd,
By fits he's temp'rate and by fits he's wild ;
But desp'rate grown, at length, with phrensied might
He strives to make a passage for the light ;

* They have an idea that the spirit wanders, when released from the body not according to general nature.

His congregated pow'rs in one last effort tries;
But foil'd, and foil'd again, gripes fast the stones and dies.

And is this all?—Oh, would to Heaven it were!
What shall with eastern Piracy compare?
Where the swarth plund'rers skulk along the main,
To whom Compassion ever pleads in vain;
Whose savage hearts no higher pleasures know,
Than the loud plaints of agonizing wo;
Who, steel'd to ev'ry more infernal crime,
Delight to taint the snowy wings of Time;
Permitting scarce one transient day to pass,
By Guilt unstain'd, thro' his perpetual glass.

Look where yon bark at distance vainly flees
From these inhuman monsters of the seas!
At first the sailors crowd their flapping sails,
To court the breeze, but ev'ry effort fails;
For soon the unrelenting foe draw near,
Brandish the sword or hurl the trusty spear:
Useless resistance, quick the pirate band
Crowd on the deck, and there exulting stand.
The captives now successive meet their fates*—
How the frame shudders whilst the pen relates!

* The cruelties practised by the Pirates upon their captives
are beyond description horrible. They never show quarter;

The trembling hand can scarce the quill sustain,
But rests awhile to ease the thongs of pain.
. . . .
Short is the respite: now it would redeem
The pen from rest, and wake anew the theme:
Cruel the tale, and tho' the Muse may weep
The savage customs practis'd on the deep;
Yet 'tis her choice those fearful deeds to sing,
And strike the lyre on a discordant string;
Tho' harsh the tone, 'tis still severely true,
And the heart sickens at the dire review.

Note the poor culprit by these hell-hounds rack'd,
With blunted knives his stiffen'd members hack'd;
His ears, his nostrils cut, and stretch'd apart,
And salt applied to aggravate the smart:
His fingers chopp'd away, and to the sore
Quick fire applied, to stop the bubbling gore;
His body pinch'd, and then allow'd repose,
Only t' endure reiterated woes:
Now pain'd anew, with points unnumber'd thrust,
Kick'd furious down, and trampled with the dust:

or, at least, very seldom. They generally put to the torture,
and derive much satisfaction from beholding the agonies of
their victims.

Life unextinguish'd, but prolong'd in pain,
To sate barbarity — how grossly vain!
A few short hours of agony when o'er,
Give the pure soul to triumph evermore.

Still be it left, alas! for me to tell
The woes inflicted by these sons of Hell*.
First is the victim ask'd, in base despite,
To scorn his God and be their proselyte.
In hopes to save his life — too crafty lure! —
He yields consent, and deems his life secure:
Delusive expectation! short it's date,
The demons smile and haste him to his fate;
Ask where he learn'd to be so pliable,
Blaspheme his tenets, call them damnable;
Spit in his eyes and smite his blister'd cheek,
Tear off his hair, and dare his tongue to speak.

Now he's suspended from the stubborn spar,
Weights at each limb, deep trench'd with many a scar;
Pull'd wide apart, excruciating wo!
The body writhing with convulsive throe!

* This is but a mere summary, and that a faint one, of the
piratical cruelties of this country.

One instant tortive, then relax'd awhile,
Each face around enlighten'd by a smile!—
Nor will the mangled suff'rer's torture cease,
Till Death's approach shall give eternal peace.
Ere life expires he ceases not to pray,
That Terror's King may bear his soul away,
To where no tyrants the fell rack prepare,
Where bliss unmarr'd abidès, for God is there:—
But all his supplications are despis'd,
The more he prays the more he is chastis'd:
These rude tormentors grinning in his face,
Give him to taste of ev'ry vile disgrace;
Laugh at his groanings, mock his piercing cries,
And send their dev'lish clamours to the skies;
Daub him with dirt, and ev'ry moan he makes
Increase their yells, till all the vessel shakes.

Finding, at length, life's final moment o'er,
And that the sufferer can feel no more,
The corpse is spurn'd, and o'er the vessel's lee
Cast, with a brutal curse, into the sea.
Thus all at last an equal doom receive;
From these* is never granted a reprieve

* The Pirates.

Unless some captive, by despair urg'd on,
To blast those joys by desp'rate triumph won,
Rous'd by revenge and certainty of death,
To send these swarthy fiends to realms beneath,
Should seize a brand and give the fabric fire,
Till all in one sad destiny expire : —
Then victors, vanquish'd, innocent and just,
Would yield to fate, and sink to baser dust;
All overpow'r'd by a superior foe,
Who never strikes but Fate ordains the blow.
Yet 'tis too rare such punishment is giv'n
By the all-just dispensing hand of Heav'n.
Uncheck'd these monsters prowl, and ev'ry day
Practise unheard-of tortures on their prey.

Oh, India! and is such the race you boast?
Do nought but robbers dwell upon thy coast?
Is thine the land where philanthropic Heav'n
Such valued bliss, such plenitude has giv'n?
Where meekest Peace has e'er caress'd her dove,
And Concord taught her fav'rite sons to love?
This where the golden Age has been restor'd,
And ev'ry thing is seen to be ador'd?
Where all is lovely as her azure skies,
Where Goodness reigns, whilst Evil sullen flies?

Is this the region where kind Nature's hand
Has been so lavish ? This the wondrous land
Where Providence such bland indulgence shows,
And fruitful Eden's choicest treasure grows?
Where, undisturb'd by Superstition's frown,
Religion's adorable rites are known ?

   Oh! empty, foolish, vain, fallacious thought!
How oft is man in Falsehood's meshes caught!
How oft beguil'd, how cheated, how deceiv'd,
When pure unblemish'd Truth is disbeliev'd !
How frequently by follies all his own,
Fated to vent Affliction's sullen moan ;
To mark Life's track, bewilder'd and distrest,
Care's heavy burthen weighing on his breast ;
In rough disquiet all his days to waste,
His restless bosom poison'd by distaste ! ——
Frail man ! but by experience never wise,
I shrink to note thy frequent miseries !
For, as I pause to mark the course of Wo,
How oft she frowns, how vast her sway below ;
My harass'd bosom palpitates anew,
And sickens at th' imaginary view.

   India ! tho' blazon'd by the trump of Fame,
Hateful delusion lurks beneath thy name !

Wide o'er thy fields Oppression's sons display
Their blood-polluted banners to the day;
Let Superstition loose, and with her aid
Make all thy swarthy progeny afraid.

   Where will be found o'er Earth's extent a race,
So seldom good, so generally base?
Who, to propitiate some monstrous god,
Cast them oft prone before Affliction's rod;
Calmly enduring — of fanatic mind —
The keenest tortures that can vex mankind!
Some, whilst the goading hook* their bodies wound,
Suspended high from the polluted ground,
Sing to their gods; nor manifesting pain,
Whirl swiftly round, forbidden to complain.
Others themselves the needful rice deny,
Till Fate's stern minister advances nigh,
Then eat by slow degrees; until at length,
Endued awhile with renovated strength;
But fast anew as soon as strength arrives,
And thus in joyless penance waste their lives.

  * Some of the Fakeer tribe, by way of penance, allow a
tenter-hook to be passed under the sinews of the back; and,
being suspended over a slow fire, remain for some considerable
time swinging; and, with apparent unconcern, address themselves to their gods in some sacred song.

Many there are, who, resolute to die,
Before the holy car extended lie;
Till o'er their frames the pond'rous axles roll,
And a brief passage open for the soul.
Some may be seen to plunge in frozen snow,
And thus await th' annihilating blow:
Frequent there are who seek the Ganges' wave,
And Death's most dreary horrors madly brave;
Leap in the hunger'd alligator's jaws,
To gain an idol'd deity's applause!

Here shall I cease this undelighting strain,
And to my early subject turn again.
Ind's horrors now shall slumber unreveal'd,
All but the few which have not been conceal'd.
Did I but briefly venture to retrace
All the fell customs of this phrensied race;
The horrible vicissitudes of ill,—
Volumes at least the narrative would fill.

END OF THE FIFTH PART.

THE CADET.

Part the Sixth.

TENACIOUS Mem'ry sickens to explore
The countless horrors of an Indian shore,—
Therefore be now my early theme pursued,
And his distress or happiness review'd,
Who leaves the land where Life's effulgent light
Drew him from plastic Nature's dreary night.

He who in torrid realms existence wastes,
Of Comfort's crystal vessel seldom tastes :

Parted from all by whom his breast was warm'd,
Whose words instructed and whose presence charm'd;
And having pass'd in Ind a length of years,
Finds nought but sorrow unassuag'd by tears:
From place to place in search of rest he hies,
But constant discontent behind him flies:
He views the various terrors of the clime,
Terrors which mock the mightiest pow'rs of rhyme;
Nor ever knows to whom he can unbend
His burthen'd heart, for here he finds no friend:
Secret within do all his sorrows rest,
And swell to drear disquietude his breast:
If e'er perchance a spark of joy be found,
Short it's duration; like a distant sound,
That momentary strikes upon the ear,
It dies away, and substitutes a tear;
Leaves an increase of pressure on the heart,
As salt assists the wounded body's smart.
Sometimes his thoughts directed to that Isle,
Where Fear suggests he ne'er again may smile;
Draw from his inmost soul the gloomy sigh,
Extort a pang, and crystallize the eye:
Imagination ne'er her pow'r denies,
But vivid colours to the draught supplies:
In her bright mirror oft he's given to see
The dear lov'd members of his family: —

But now the contrast with his earlier day
Quick forms, and sweeps the transient joy away *.
Sometimes — the greatest curse that can befall,
That from the bosom drains it's blackest gall—
Should wealth reward his exile — he's a mark
For some fair market Miss — some masked shark ;
And yields, perhaps, in unpropitious hour,
To lead the maid to Hymen's sombrest bow'r;
Gives her, with kind intent, the name of wife,
And casts a canker on his rest for life.
Now she, that once on homeliest dishes fed,
And slept o' nights in an uncurtain'd bed,

---

* Such are supposed to be the natural feelings of a man,
whom the chance of destiny has fixed in a country to which he
could never reconcile himself. Such feelings, it is presumed,
would naturally operate on a susceptible mind, reduced to a
state of melancholy by being far situated from a home, from
relations, from friends, and all that can be considered valuable
in this brief existence. Many are there in India, beyond a
doubt, who appear to enjoy themselves and live in sufficient
content; but it is a content that more refined philosophy
would spurn at: time probably renders them callous to earlier
regret; and, although they would eagerly return to their own
country, they drown all their dearer wishes in baser pursuits—
the chase and the bottle. They quell frequently the more
exquisite emotions of the heart, and live in unsatisfactory in-
difference.

VOL. I.   L

Lolls on a couch or in her palankeen,
Giddy with ale or stupified with spleen;
Mounts her barouche and scours the esplanade,
And smiling bows to Col'nel on parade.
She views her injur'd spouse with careless eyes,
Insults his wo and mocks his frequent sighs;
Coquets with ev'ry youth of comely face,
And leaves her husband's honour in disgrace *;
Hies to some *friend*, and there engag'd in play,
Runs o'er the common scandal of the day;
Games till the crow begins his early tune,
Then goes to bed and sleeps till after noon.

Thus the poor husband, ev'ry care of life
Augmented by the follies of his wife,

* As has been before intimated, many women of low birth
contrive to come to this country. Frequently they are suffi-
ciently successful to deceive some unfortunate man, who has
enough to afford them a handsome maintenance; and, when
once covered by the shield of marriage, give loose to the
natural inclinations of their hearts; little solicitous about their
own reputations, or the credit and happiness of their husbands.
However, let me be just enough to say, that I do not for a
moment doubt of there being many, very many, estimable
women in India, although some among them are widely distant
from *good* fame.

Finds no quiescence; ev'ry hast'ning year
Serves but to make his anguish more severe:
Sometimes the chase may be a while pursued,
To blunt the pangs of sorrow unsubdued;
There, 'neath a fervent sun, o'er forest hoar,
And steril plain, he hunts the sturdy boar;
Urges his foaming steed in swift career,
Till gasps the tusked monster 'neath his spear;
And, rising with life's latest effort, tries
To charge; but falling, chafes the plain and dies.
The day's sport ended, here awhile be view'd
What hateful course of pleasure is pursued.

His boon companions all, if boon they be,
Prepare to spend the night in jollity;
And, dinner ended, large libations pour'd
To Bacchus' altar, load the groaning board;
Around the merry toast is constant giv'n,
With roars that mock the thunder peals of Heav'n;
To the last drop successive cups they drain,
Nor empty long permitted to remain:
Laughter and riot fill the spreading tent
With all the noisier din of merriment* :

* When a party goes hog hunting, a tent is always sent for-
ward to the ground, for eating and sleeping in, as the chase is

Drunk at the last to bed each rev'ller hies,
And like a fatting hog obscenely lies.
He who, to shun a wife's dull, cold embrace,
Essay'd the better pleasures of the chase,
From the foul scene his eyes disgusted turns,
And Dissipation's proffer'd goblet spurns;
Reseeks his home, where nought of comfort's known,
The store-house of afflictions all his own;
Where—the eternal torment of his life—
He hears the constant gabble—of his wife.
At length, beneath the rigours of the clime,
Enervate, wasted, in life's rudest prime
He dies, perhaps unmourn'd; and finds a tomb
'Mid some drear wild, or forest's distant gloom,
Where roams the lion, where the tiger prowls;
Where snakes repose, or where the gaunt wolf howls;
Where human foot has scarcely ever trod;
Where pois'nous reptiles sport along the sod;

generally renewed every morning for some five or six days
together. When the sport of the day is ended, a dinner of the
slain boar is dressed; the head at the top of the table; on
which the party regale after the fatigues of hunting; and
generally spend the remaining part of the evening in riot and
enjoying the festal pleasures of the bottle. The chase in this
country is certainly a most dissipated pleasure.

Where the fell jackal, skulking for his prey,
Scrapes the fresh earth and bears the corpse away;
Devours that vast machine which God did form,
And of it's right defrauds the hungry worm.

Yes! in this region, oft the barren wild
Receives the relics of Misfortune's child:
And, but few hours elaps'd, here mourn ye brave,
Remains no vestige of the soldier's grave!
The dead, but lately animated clay,
From it's last tenement is borne away;
Whilst the bleach'd fragments of the bones remain,
Pounc'd by the sun, upon the blasted plain;
And, till to dust the osseous remnants waste,
By ev'ry heedless trav'ller's foot disgrac'd *.

'Tis but too oft, in these dominions wide,
That the most harsh calamities are tried:

---

* Many there are, no doubt, who pretend to ridicule the idea
of solicitude about the treatment of the body after death, and
say it is matter of little consequence how it is bestowed:—in
the name of Indecency, let the bodies of such be thrown to the
dogs. They would think nothing the worse of India if the
bodies of all who visit it were buried in wilds, and eaten by
beasts of prey.

Nor ye who read this sad recital deem,
That 'tis the fabrication of a dream:—
Truth stands confess'd, and tho' severe her tone,
Dulls the broad glare of Falsehood's specious zone.

Ye who are nourish'd at Profusion's breast,
Whom sullen griefs nor fiercer cares molest;
Who all the fleeting hours of life beguile
In household cares, where bliss rewards the toil,
Blush not to own a momentary pain,
Nor be Misfortune's pleadings heard in vain:
Mock not at chaste Compassion's earnest call,
And let the sympathizing droplet fall;
'Tis Pity's emblem, to misfortune due,
The heart's best balm when angry woes pursue.

How often here, when Sol destructive reigns,
And sucks the ruddy moisture from the veins,
Haggard disease upon the frame descends,
And pain corporeal to Affliction lends;
Corrupts the liver, swells the heaving side,
And mocks each cure by sage experience tried;
Forms the vast abscess in the swelling lobe,
And to it's cure invites the pointed probe:—
But vain all trial of the surgeon's skill,
When Death is nigh to work th' Almighty's will.

Tremble ye Parents at this piteous tale!
Beware ye have not equal cause to wail,
With those now doom'd in anguish to deplore
An offspring's fate, on Ind's uncertain shore:
Giv'n to the dust unwept, nor e'en a pray'r
Breath'd o'er the corse, for friendship was not there.

How often here his nature man belies!—
Polluting influence of eastern skies!
The feelings of humanity expire,
As, quench'd by water, dies the stubborn fire.
Self is sole monarch; loud exults the heart,
When HE, o'er life supreme, directs his dart:
Joy jocund smiles on ev'ry waning breath,
For Int'rest rises by the aid of Death.
Oh shame! in India when a fellow dies*,
The sparks of triumph glisten in the eyes!

* However shocking to humanity it may appear, and however it may derogate from the exalted character of a Christian,
it is, nevertheless, precisely thus. The death of an officer
must (unless he be of very short standing in the army) leave
a vacancy, which affords a step to every person below him in
the regiment. All who thus benefit rejoice at the circumstance which procures them such advantage: consequently
there are generally found more who rejoice at, than who
bewail, the death of an officer. It is a common practice to

Parents ! — forgive the Muse — be warn'd in time,
Nor trust your children to an eastern clime;
For, once convey'd beyond the Indian main,
The sire and child may never meet again.
Few are allow'd — such Destiny's decree —
To traverse back the circumscribing sea:
For one who lives the homeward wave to try,
('Tis well attested,) fifty often die.
Whilst he, who, thinking all his sorrows past,
Seeks a lov'd home, finds no content at last:
The customs new, the manners all unknown,
He almost doubts the land to be his own:
A foreigner complete, of alter'd mind,
He looks with eye of wonder on mankind;
Where'er he turns dull Disappointment hies,
Mars lovely Hope, and the foil'd cherub flies,
Leaving a dreary void around the heart,
Where Grief had long-time aim'd it's sharpest dart.

pass the pen through the names of those in the yearly register
who are sickly, and appear likely to die in the course of a
short time. I have seen registers, of which every officer generally has one, quite defaced by these marks. The most
favourite toast amongst the military in this country is :—" A
bloody war and a sickly season."

Alas! what blessings is he giv'n to know—
Long cast upon the rocky coast of wo—
Who, after twenty years of sorrow fled,
Speeds to his home to rest his hoary head?
Sad is the question; whilst escapes the sigh,
The heart's emotion glistens in the eye.
Tho' young in years, in constitution old,
His body worn by ailings manifold;
Sadly infirm, and wasted by disease;
His temper cross and difficult to please,
Something he finds, in ev'ry passing hour,
To foil Contentment's salutary pow'r.

There is a kind of chaos of the mind,
When, all the blunter faculties refin'd,
By quick'ning Sorrow in collision meet,
And almost hurry Reason from her seat;
Each fierce emotion struggling hard for sway—
All in the mental hold tumultuous play.

Suppose at last arriv'd the man of woes
To England's shores, in search of kind repose;
He seeks his friends, but friends can find no more,
All having reach'd an everlasting shore:
Around he gazes, still his searching eye
Looks o'er a *stranger'd* world, nor can descry,

Amid the various crowd, one object dear,
Whom he could bid his harass'd heart revere.
The lov'd companious of his earliest day
Afar dispers'd, or sunk in dust away;
His relatives belov'd, or gone or dead,
Strangers sprung up and living in their stead.
Now waste his days, one sad unvarying scene,
And scarce a transient hour glides by serene.
From place to place in search of ease he hies,
But still Grief's constant shaft against him flies;
And seldom can a lenitive be found
T' allay the ceaseless anguish of the wound.
He seeks the social board, the crowded court*,
Where Peers and Commoners alike resort;
Or to behold upon the mimic stage
The tragic beauties of our Shakspeare's page;
Takes him where Siddons' rare dramatic pow'rs
Throw a sweet charm upon our murder'd hours: —
Yet all avails not, discontented still,—
He feels the sad supremacy of ill:
Yet from himself is impotent to flee,
For in himself lies all his misery!
Thus, where he hop'd the highest bliss to gain,
He only meets with aggravated pain.

* The racket court.

The land which once his Infancy ador'd,
Where Nature loves to ope her choicest hoard;
Where he was wont in earlier youth to stray,
As Peace bestow'd her desultory ray;
Where Education to his pliant mind
Convey'd what only can adorn mankind,
And taught the buds of intellect to bloom,
And drew the blossom forth from infant gloom—
The land,—which furnish'd all his joy before,
Now to his heart can furnish joy no more.
What pangs with earlier recollection rise,
And to the cup of Grief add fresh supplies!

Too true, alas! that lov'd paternal Isle,
Where infant Nature gave him first to smile,
Now, to *his* eye, of ev'ry charm divest,
No longer proves to him a home of rest.

When just preparing, five long lustrums o'er,
To bid adieu to India's blasting shore,
He feels, perhaps, some transitory bliss,
In counting joys he thinks may soon be his.—
'Tis but delusion! like a hasty dream,
Or a thin cloud that breaks the lunar beam;

A moment interrupts the silvery light,
Only to give it clearer to the sight *.
Fancy too oft deceptive pictures draws,
Where ev'ry tint a pleasing union shows,
Plac'd at a distance ; — for, if view'd too near,
Her shades wax pale, her colours disappear :
So the poor worm, that trims his lamp by night,
No longer shines when brought before the light.

Fancy doth oft a pow'rful influence own,
Glads for a while, then gives the soul to moan :
Sometimes the placid garb of Peace she'll wear,
Then change, and take the vestments of Despair ;
As many forms as Proteus she'll assume,
Wear Age's furrows or Youth's smirking bloom ;
One while in kind Contentment's vesture clad,
Soft she'll advance and bid the heart be glad ;
Then closely rob'd in dark Misfortune's dress,
Stand up the dauntless foe of Happiness.

Oft as her flutt'ring wings in artful play
Beguile the first encumb'ring hours away ; —

* When the moon bursts from behind a cloud, to the eye
there appears a stronger light than was reflected from her orb
before it was hid ; naturally occasioned by the instant tran-
sition from gloom to an unobstructed light.

When the worn exile, in Joy's fancied hour,
Seeking his home, admits her various pow'r;
She bids fond Expectation lend a smile,
Lightens the heart and glads it for a while;
Gives interesting visions * to the mind,
Castles in air, which vanish with the wind:
For, when the plausible delusion flies,
And gives it's place to drear realities,
The pageant phantom quits the easy brain,
Nor ever there again assumes her reign:
Truth, tho' severe, begins her peerless sway,
And plucks the trim Deceiver's robes away;
Proclaims aloud the cares to mortals giv'n,
And tells that Bliss is only found in Heav'n.

He who has pass'd twice thirteen † rounds of time
'Mid all the horrors of a scorching clime;
Tann'd by a rigid sun's enerving ray,
And Sorrow's block plac'd in Life's broadest way;
His constitution undermin'd and worn,
His frame by fierce Disease's tenters torn,

* It is, I believe, a frequent case for old *British* Indians, when on the eve of returning to England, to fancy it every thing that can be supposed to be delightful; and often, on their arrival, find themselves disappointed in every particular.

† Twenty-five years is the time allotted for an officer in the native armies to remain in India.

Finds seldom a quiescent hour at last,
To compensate the anguish of the past;
But to his land paternal frequent hies,
Looks for Content, and disappointed—dies.

When safe return'd to England's wish'd for coast,
Where Hope had told Affliction would be lost,
Shows Disappointment oft an aspect drear,
Harrows the heart to agony severe;
Implants a thorn corrosive in the breast,
Which rankles there and robs it of it's rest.
The long lorn wand'rer, after years of toil,
Finds he's an alien on his native soil;
No grateful friend to welcome his return,
Or draw forth joy from Gratulation's urn;
His only *consolation* to deplore
The baneful indiscretion* done of yore;
To pause how oft he's combated with woes,
Hoping in peace his latter hours to close;
Thinking in life's elapsing day to rest
His aged head on Friendship's succ'ring breast:—
Sadly deceiv'd, at length to fate resign'd,
To nobler weal he points his harass'd mind:
A few short months pass on in dull career,
When Nature bursts the narrow limit here;

---

* In leaving his home for India.

Eternity's dark curtain pulls aside,
And casts the soul upon it's doubtful tide.

Years spent in exile, all he finds at home,
A wretched end, a miserable tomb.

THE END.

ODE TO ADVERSITY.

[Written in India.]

I.

RUDE nurse of Wo! does hallow'd Virtue's voice
 Calm those dark horrors flashing from thine eye?
Didst e'er thou bid the sufferer rejoice,
 Soften his grief or wipe the tear-drop dry?
 No! stern is thy dominion, harsh Adversity!

II.

When Expectation, in delighting guise,
 Points out the phantom Peace, perceiv'd afar,
We feed but upon *dream'd* realities:—
 Awak'ning soon we see what fools we are,
 And, in the stead of Bliss, mount Sorrow's rusty car.

III.

Haggard Adversity! thy grizzly mien
   Quashes the finer feelings of the soul;
Casts a drear gloom on Life's uncertain scene,
   And bends the stubborn heart to thy controul:
   Warm as the solar ray, or frigid as the Pole.

IV.

'Tis thou dost quench the glowing fires that burn
   Within the breast where Love has pour'd his balm:
Thou dost the noblest projects overturn,
   And chase the bosom's beatific calm,
   Leaving too frequent there irremeable qualm.

V.

Unsightly Parent of ungenial Care,
   Leave not thy sombre rule to work me ill!
Fly far, distressful fost'rer of Despair!—
   I dread to bend to thy uncourtly will,
   Though it be Fate's harsh mandate that thou dost fulfil.

TO MY DOG.

[Written in India.]

―――――

I.

SOCIAL companion of my doleful hours,
  Grateful thy genuine gratitude I see:
Tho' unendow'd with Reason's nobler pow'rs,
  Still there's in man less friendship than in thee.

II.

Should hostile feet my humble doors invade,
  Thine active courage keeps at bay the foe;
Or should the snake steal deathful from the glade,
  Thou risk'st thy life to ward the horrid wo.

III.

Where 'mongst the sons of Pleasure shall be found
  One of such worth, so estimably giv'n?
Ne'er shall I know on earth a friend so sound,
  And for a kinder I must trust to Heav'n.

TO THE POPPY.

[Written in India.]

Flow'r of Oblivion! emblem meet of Death!
    I pluck thee tremblingly!
Dull thoughts arise—suspends my humid breath—
    I view thee feelingly!

The grief-worn wretch doth thy assistance crave
    In hours of misery:
Thou art, dull flow'r! a peopler of the grave—
    Life's subtle enemy!

Thine opiate proves a not unfrequent guide
    To drear Eternity:
Sad deleterious plant! too often tried
    By sons of infamy!

But still thy value must we not disown,
    To Sorrow lenitive :
Thou forcest Slumber oft-times from his throne,
    Wo's frequent sanative.

To Good and Evil thou'rt alike allied,
    O plant unlovely !
Thou art the Hemlock's stern unsocial bride,
    And scarce more goodly.

STANZAS.

[Written in India.]

Ye callous worldlings! ye who cry
　'Gainst Love's celestial sway,
Who mock at Sensibility,
　And turn in scorn away;
Rais'd not for you the lowly strain,
　'Tis sung to Beauty's ear—
E'en Orpheus' lyre were tun'd in vain,
　Had such as you been near.

Forbear ye Prudes, long mark'd by age,
　With wrinkles, spleen, and spite,
To vent on Youth your churlish rage,
　Where Love begets delight!

For you, ye frigid, bearded Maids,
　The sigh was never heav'd —
Now go and mumble *o'er your beads,*
　Of ev'ry hope bereav'd :

And learn, tho' in Life's latter stage,
　That tenderness of heart
Is priz'd in ev'ry gen'rous age :
　But learn it to your smart,
That had ye felt as others feel,
　To whom Love's pow'r is known,
On earth ye might have found a *Heav'n,*
　Now *Hell** is all your own.

* The vestal sisterhood are said to lead Apes in Hell.

AN

ODE TO MELANCHOLY.

[Written in India.]

―――――

" How blest the Solitary's lot,
" Who, all forgetting, all forgot
    " Within this humble cell ;
" The cavern wild, with tangling roots,
" Sits o'er his newly gather'd fruits,
    " Beside his crystal well !
" Or haply to his ev'ning thought,
    " By unfrequented stream,
" The ways of men are distant brought,
    " A faint-collected dream."

BURNS.

―――――

I.

DAUGHTER of Sorrow ! Melancholy, hail !
    How sweet a solace oft thine influence lends
    To solitary wo ! — The heart unbends
And pensive Pleasure smiles. — For ever hail,
        Thou lenitive to pain !
        My soul assents thy reign,
    Calm, altho' sad, and impotent to wail.

II.

When Night enshrouds the circumjacent globe,
  And young Endymion's soft admirer sheds
  Her radiant light below: — in verdant meads,
Where Nature wears Spring's plain but lovely robe,
    Does Melancholy dwell;
    Whilst from her mossy cell
Attractive Meditation lightly treads.

III.

The sisters meet, and solemn Thought is rous'd!
  The mind roams pond'ring thro' her trackless maze.
  Life's brittle prop, it's various beaten ways,
The woes to which Mortality's espous'd
    Pass in succinct review —
    The bosom throbs anew,
As recollections rise of happier days.

IV.

An awful contrast this with earlier time,
  When mirthful Boyhood frolick'd unrestrain'd,
  When by Grief's scourge the breast was never pain'd,
And even thought untarnish'd by a crime —

I drink, alas! too deep
At Mem'ry's fount.—Oh sleep,
Sleep Recollection—cease thy pow'r sublime*!

V.

As soon might Argus erst have tried to close
  His hundred eyes, or Cerberus have slept;—
  As soon the fabled Dragon, too, who kept
The mystic apples, might have sought repose;
    For Mem'ry never still
    Hath unrestricted will,
And dwells alike on happiness or woes.

VI.

Thy tardy finger, Melancholy, draws
  The recent map of Life's vicissitudes:
  When on the mind thine influence intrudes,
It rests awhile to ponder Nature's laws,
    Explores this mortal span
    Of transitory man,
And wakes the heart to sad similitudes.

* I think that I may venture, without holding any consultation with the metaphysicians, to pronounce Memory one of the sublimest among the intellectual faculties.

VII.

To quick Remembrance frequently arise
  The drear misfortunes of departed years;
  Whilst Melancholy's voice provokes the tears
Of keen regret —but, pointing to the skies,
     Bids Fancy picture there,
     Impregnable by care,
Those once belov'd partaking heav'nly joys *.

VIII.

Oft when the heart by Love 's severely torn,
  She sooths the troubled passions into calm;
  To ev'ry fest'ring wound applies a balm,
And from the breast plucks Grief's corroding thorn.
     The softest beauties grace
     Her mild expressive face,
By Virtue foster'd and from Virtue † born.

* Alluding to the loss of a father and mother.

† Melancholy is here considered as a calm and acquiescent resignation to the Divine Will, not a sullen insensibility to the afflictions to which mortality is frequently allied: on the contrary, a mild regret, supported by a holy reliance on the justness of a beneficent Creator's providence.

IX.

Ask what is Life, it's unsubstantial joys?
  The transient passing of a gloomy cloud!
  The swathe is made but just before the shroud;
And, whilst felicity the mind employs,
      How oft man's peerless foe
      Directs th' annihilating blow,
Whilst soon the worm his foul remains destroys.

X.

Thus Melancholy whisp'ring, gives the soul
  To mild religious musing; blunts each throe,
  That springs from keen ungovernable wo,
And brings it under dignified controul.
      Where'er the vestal hies,
      The breast she purifies,
And points beyond where mortal thought can go.

XI.

Come, then; meek blue-eyed Melancholy, come!
  Quench all the fire of anguish in my breast,
  Lull ev'ry strong emotion into rest,
And make it Resignation's silent home!
      I woo thee, placid maid,
      I seek thy noiseless shade!
Then come, meek blue-eyed Melancholy, come!

AN

IRREGULAR ODE

ON

THE MISERIES OF HUMAN EXISTENCE.

[Written in India.]

STROPHE THE FIRST.

WHEN Nature opens the fructif'rous womb,
And gives existence to the future man,
She ushers him where griping Care,
The foster parent of Despair,
May, arm'd with galling pains, molest
And render rough his passage to the tomb.
Here, when a few brief years their course have ran,
His placid, unencumber'd breast—
But lately throbbing unopprest,
Which evinc'd peace ere Reason's sense began—

May, in some unexpected moment, know
The most severe vicissitudes of wo!
Accord indulgent Progeny of Jove;
Who PÆAN's vast supremacy alone
Acknowledg'd chief o'er song, art wont to own —
Your votive aid, and from those bow'rs above,
Where, in Elysium's consecrated grove
Your footsteps tread
The verdant mead,
That carpets where ye dwell;
Strike the symphonious shell,
And let the gradual cadence flow,
In modulation smooth and slow,
For what alike with harmony can plead!

STROPHE THE SECOND.

What is the busy world with it's turmoil?
A vasty show, where various puppets play;
And, having rioted their hours away,
Again commingle with their kindred soil,
To fat their parent clay.
'Tis here Man springs to life,
And, whilst he clamours loud for bliss,
Cares and calamities are his,
For ever, ever rife

Bounds along seductive Pleasure,
Filling oft Affliction's measure,
After Joy; despiteful Sorrow
Sudden bids a sad good morrow,
And in Pleasure's track abides;
Waiting there to take her spring,
When keen Suspicion shall have droop'd his wing,
And gores Contentment's sides.
When mild Mirth, of aspect bland,
Join'd with Laughter hand in hand,
Permits the heart to taste of peace,
The lurking foe her crest uprears,
O'erburthen'd and deform'd by fears,
And bids the breast it's milder throbbings cease.

EPODE THE FIRST.

Where shall mortal eye discover,
Tho' it search Creation over,
Content uninfluenc'd by Pain?
Here unrelenting Poverty we view,
With all her haggard and unseemly crew,
That—like a dun wolf's brood,
Their jaws distain'd with blood—

Ne'er quit the lank grim parent's track,
But yelling, follow on amain,
And, pressing closely on her back,
Benignant QUIETUDE of MIND pursue;
Till the rous'd cherub, chas'd afar,
Shuns, in swift flight, th' unequal war;
And all attempts at repossession prove but vain.
But is it those alone whom wealth allures,
Whom potent gold from public taunt secures,
That feel the throbs of conscience cease,
And harbour never dying peace?
Can sordid pelf exonerate misdeed?
No, spite of all, the guilty heart must bleed!
Do those whom wealth endows, alone
Sit steadfast on Contentment's throne?
No, no, alas! how very frequent these,
Gnaw'd by the rigid grinders of disease,
Groan, inly groan their dreary hours away,
To manifold anxieties a prey.
The sons of MAMMON hourly know
Affliction's oft-repeated throe!—
Perhaps a wife, an only infant dies!
Can gold restore them?—Dross, mere dross,
That doth the venal mind engross,
But ne'er can ward approaching miseries.

ANTISTROPHE THE FIRST.

Thou by purer Pleasure ne'er carest,
What seekest thou to make thee blest?
Do " parts allure thee ?" ponder on his doom *;
Who, spurn'd by Fortune, bow'd him to the tomb;
Barr'd from companions, relatives and friends
Over whose melancholy bier
Was dropt no sympathetic tear,
Whose life was an alternate scene
Of cloudy and serene;
Whose latter days were gloom'd by woes severe,
For which no ray of genius made amends.
By a mother disown'd,
Neglected, despis'd,
By fortune chastis'd,
In affliction he groan'd,
The best, the noblest, most resplendent day
Of evanescent life, forlorn, away.
Where did the bard expire whose Muse sublime
Shall sound her tuneful trump to farthest time ?—-
Here, with mild Pity, Indignation blends—
He died in gaol, untarnish'd by a crime.
Deem not that in possessing parts alone,
The most unsullied happiness is known;.

* Savage.

For those too oft of most elastic mind,
Too proud to truckle to a meaner ill,
Spread their fine wings upon Ambition's wind,
And at the last Affliction's current swill.

ANTISTROPHE THE SECOND.

Is it from Love that quietude is gain'd?
The tyrant god his venom'd arrow wings,
Till the too effervescent bosom's pain'd;
And pain'd sometimes by fell Remorse's stings.
It heaves incessant then with troublous throe,
And finds that from expected joys
Results the most insufferable woe.
She who the sentient heart decoys
May be no angél — who can tell?—
'Tis Matrimony breaks the spell,
And gives the pair or pain or bliss to know.
Beauty — a transient gloss that lives awhile
Beneath the witching covert of a smile,
But which the breath of Time destroys —
Directs Love's enervating dart
Against the unsuspecting heart;
But, 'neath the cherub mask she sometimes bears,
Evil too oft her tatter'd banner rears;

And, when young Hymen's Gordian knot is tied,
Plucks quickly down the flimsy cheat,
And gives, unscreen'd by shrewd Deceit,
Just as she is, the chaste imagin'd bride.
Does thought of Fame delight thee? Where expir'd
He, whose dramatic Muse sublimely high
Scatter'd profuse the flow'rs of Poesy?
He *, by Pieria's buskin'd dame inspir'd,
Thro' want and hunger clos'd in death his eye.
Can loud Renown from Death, Disease, or Pain,
From Malice or Reproach, her vot'ry save?
Oft Envy, springing from her dark domain,
Calls on loud Scandal, her obsequious slave,
And blasts with Falsehood's trump an honourable name,
Where well approv'd Desert had wreath'd eternal fame.
Does rank with titles happiness secure?
Here oft the bark of Obloquy is heard,
Whilst foul and vehement Disgrace
Uprears his many spotted face,
And on the Reputation casting slurs impure,
Excites rebellious Wo, and plucks chaste Honour's beard.
Bliss is with Rank unfrequently allied!
This is, too oft, the fosterer of Pride,
A deadly foe to Peace, of empire insecure.

* Otway.

EPODE THE SECOND.

Mark where the fawning Parasite now stands,
Close at the titled Mortal's sculptur'd gate,
To court the dull caresses of the GREAT!
Does pure unblemish'd Joy with those join hands,
On whom the Peer bestows his smile?
No; Independence' tongue the while
Declares it mean
Against the gilded props of Pow'r to lean;
Bright Honour startles, bursts the venal chain,
And scorns Dependence, spite of ev'ry pain.
Have I summ'd all the ills existence knows?
What pen shall number all it's woes!
Sometimes, when visionary Bliss seems near,
A wife, a bosom friend,—ay, all we reckon dear
Is in one moment ravish'd from our eyes,
And Hope o'erwhelm'd by potent miseries.
Nor is it rare to find some poor forlorn,
A rigid Parent's undeserving scorn;
From a rude home discarded to essay
The rigours rife on Life's encumber'd way.
Few are the joys allotted here below,
Earth is the constant dwelling-house of Wo,

Where man must buffet 'gainst incessant ill,
To make his soul more worthy that abode,
Where, if deserving, he shall meet his God,
And bend in endless blessing to th' Almighty will.

EPITAPH

ON

A FEMALE INFANT.

THE snow-drop, offspring of a rigid sire,
Cradled in storms, protrudes it's spotless head;
But oft as soon as born is doom'd t' expire,
One moment blooming and the next struck dead.
Thus — pull'd by want to life — untimely died
The beauteous babe — to earth but shortly giv'n,
When Death secur'd the infant as his bride,
And plac'd it's spotless soul aloft in Heav'n.

A QUERY.

I WONDER where shall now be found
To answer what I here propound?
  I'll vouch against it, no man;
Why Adam did at first proclaim,
So awful and so dread a name,
  For that sweet creature—*Wo! Man!*

ANSWER.

'TWERE hard indeed, I must allow,
To fix exact the reason now,
  But guessing's not uncivil:
Did not our sire primordial, know
That Woman, soon or late, would go
  Advising — with the Devil?

A

𝕭𝖗𝖎𝖊𝖋 𝕾𝖐𝖊𝖙𝖈𝖍

OF

THE ISLAND OF MADEIRA,

AND

ITS INHABITANTS.

[Written during a short residence there, on my way out to
India, in the year of our Lord 1810.]

" Vilius argentum est auro, virtutibus aurum."
HORACE.

HERE shall an artless Muse her aid extend,
And what she can to dull Description lend:
Her pow'r, tho' insufficient to rehearse
What might demand the noblest force of verse;
Still her less vig'rous efforts would she try,
To cull some simpler flow'rs of Poesy;

But, if those efforts prove to be no use,
A stripling's song may sure expect excuse.

Tho' 'twill be vain to make attempt to soar,
Or grace my subject with sublimer lore ;
Still, if I dress it in the garb of Truth,
I trust to 'scape the wound from Censure's tooth.

A land unpolish'd I'd attempt to paint,
Where foul Pollution spreads it's grossest taint,
Where fell Ferocity, with sightless eyes,
Sends Virtue sorrowing to her native skies ;
Where Gorgon Cruelty, abortive child
Of Superstition, wanders unrevil'd ;
Where Superstition, blind to Reason's light,
Locks up the mind in Error's tenfold night ;
Where savage Pride his pompous wand protends,
And from the heart it's brightest beauties rends ;
Where brutal Ignorance triumphant reigns,
And trusts to Avarice her sordid gains ;
Where Imposition dwells in hateful ease,
And where Corruption aggravates Disease.

Here may be found, by grinning Guilt defil'd,
The murd'rous parent, the felonious child :

Here thro' the streets the nightly plund'rer hies,
And robs the straggler of his last supplies;
Then draws the keen stiletto from his breast,
And sends his soul to seek eternal rest.
Oft, when in casual argument engag'd,
The fierce Polemic, not to be assuag'd,
Draws from his poke the sanguinary knife,
And thrusts it fearless at the source of life;
Looks on his late companion's corse, the while
His rugged features tortur'd to a smile.
No laws to stop the prevalence of Ill,
Each harden'd villain executes his will;
Spreads squalid Guilt's polluted banners wide,
And takes his daily station at their side;
Incessant with the monster strives to dwell,
And for himself secures the meed of Hell.

I witness'd here what never met mine eyes
In any land where man's reputed wise;
Where Christianity has rear'd her crest,
And erring mortals with her doctrines blest.
Here ribald Vice, endued with pow'r supreme,
Floats swiftly down Corruption's fetid stream;
And as it's course along it swiftly glides,
Bears off vast numbers on it's muddy tides.

Ye weak! to moral obligation blind,
Why live a degradation to mankind?
Why, like the brutal herds that range the plain,
Expose your naked * forms to sun and rain?
Why from your bosoms strike the beauteous dove
Of social friendship, reasonable love?
Who shall declare why this unpolish'd race,
Not by the hand of Heav'n created base,
Pass on in life's career, deprav'd by crimes
Unparallel'd in Afric's rudest climes.

Ye whom the Muse reviles, how can ye give
Harbour to Guilt and in dishonour live?
Tho' gen'rous Nature pours her bounties forth,
How slightly do ye prize their — " passing worth;"
With what disgusting apathy review
Each season round, the stores she wastes for you!
Tho' all productions of the earth you boast,
And with profusion favour'd without cost,
Still ye 're in debt to Nature's hand alone,
For ye bestow no labour of your own.
No manual toil assists the rising plants,
Nor can profusion satisfy your wants.

* From what I had an opportunity of observing, the common
people wear very little covering: I have seen them on the
beach at work quite naked.

If HE who reigns omnipotent on high,
And scatters vegetation from the sky,
At each revolving season deign'd to shed
His choicest favours on each worthless head,
Such kind indulgence would in nought avail
To spur ye on to Labour's nobler pale ;
E'en then Neglect would be your sluggish choice,
Nor would abundance stifle Mis'ry's voice.
Your souls debas'd by ev'ry fouler vice,
From cheating, plund'ring, e'en to catching lice*,
Would never yield to lordly Reason's rule,
Which stops the gibing tongue of Ridicule ;
Checks the too ardent raptures of the soul,
And brings it under laudable controul ;
But like the crew of Comus would ye dance
Before the filthy shrine of Ignorance.
Too pertinacious, shallow minded fools,
At best but pallid Superstition's tools !
Dead to morality, and Virtue's foes,
Ye are yourselves the cause of all your woes !
Long be it yours to kiss the wounding rod,
The scourge of Fate, the vengeance of your God !

* A trite old adage has it, that cleanliness is next to
godliness; from which it is but reasonable to conclude, that
uncleanliness is but one remove from ungodliness.

What honest pastimes spur your hours away?
What chaste employments occupy the day?
Do sprightly recreations, healthful sport,
From toils more rigid yield a kind resort?
No, labour here to indolence is grown,
And sociable diversion 's scarcely known:
Obscenity, with foul and lep'rous brow,
Prompts your *fair* sex to imitate the sow;
Nor do the hardier less to filth incline,
But like their weaker ape the grunting swine:
Like them — luxurious ease their chief desire —
They smell at filth and wallow in the mire;
Spend hour on hour in rummaging for lice,
He most admir'd who harbours most of *price**,
Whole swarms take refuge in the matted hair,
Discharge their nits, and hatch prolific there: —
But here the Muse disgusted stops her lyre,
And hastes to strike a less discordant wire.

The Country would she now essay to sing,
Where jocund Summer joins with laughing Spring;

* Here, it must be confessed, is somewhat of caricature:
however, I have seen people in the heat of the day, sitting at
the entrances of their respective houses, lousing each other, and
many even in the streets. Whole families occupy themselves
thus frequently.

Where hoary Winter ne'er attempts to frown,
And Autumn never wears her leafless crown.
Upon this Isle doth Vegetation rear
Her flow'ry throne, and rests securely here:
Tho' Cultivation lends but little aid
To plant the garland firmly on her head,
Fertility exists 'mid Chaos wild,
And horns of Plenty o'er the land are pil'd:
Herbs and rare shrubs in one promiscuous mass
Oft vegetate, obscur'd by canes and grass;
Nor does the Idler take prudential heed
From the rich soil to pluck the cumb'ring weed.

Nought but the vines are cautiously caress'd,
From whose ripe fruit the luscious wine's express'd;
No pains are spar'd, no industry denied,
That they a fruitful gath'ring may provide:
But who can see — nor wish these fools chastis'd —
The nobler gifts of Heav'n so lightly priz'd?
Who could behold on earth neglected lie
The brightest shrubs that can regale the eye,
And not exclaim—Supreme o'er earth and skies!
Why on a race so rude bestow such rich supplies?

Here, in confusion budding, may be seen
Each stately plant that loves a clime serene:

Yet, from neglect, it fades before mature,
And none it's fruits or blossoms can procure.
The coffee-tree 'mongst others may be found,
With ev'ry shrub that loves a torrid ground:
Bananas, melons, and the luscious pine,
With all the various produce of the vine,
Grow here abundant; here their sweets protrude
In gloomy dells, on precipices rude.

Luxuriant here the fragrant orange thrives,
With ev'ry fruit that Vegetation gives;
Yet scarcely one it's best perfection gains,
Denied the lazy Cultivator's pains.
Trees, plants unnumber'd, meet th' admiring eyes,
But ev'ry tree and plant neglected lies,
And, by default of culture, shrinks and dies.

Tho' such confusion on this Island rests,
No noxious beast the gifted land molests;
No pois'nous reptile in the solar heat
Darts out destructive 'neath the trav'ller's feet:
Here may be dare to wander undismay'd,
Nor fear at noon to seek the friendly shade.

If from the bay be view'd the country round,
The vast variety that decks the ground,

No mean impression can the mind receive,
Or the too sad reality believe;
For to the sight a prospect is display'd,
Where Spring appears in all his best array'd.
Gaze on the far perspective, and admire
That hill of alpine height; like a tall spire
It's tow'ring brow it boldly rears on high,
And hides it's lofty summit in the sky;
Involving vapours rest upon it's head,
And seem to make it's ample brow their bed.

All those abrupt *excrescences*, which rear
Their bulks stupendous 'mid th' elastic air,
Tho' situate 'neath warm and trying skies,
Receive from Nature's granary supplies,
Of which no realm can make an equal boast,
From Zembla's snows to torrid Afric's coast:
They teem with ev'ry vegetative gem,
Tho' most abundant shoots the vinous stem.

When from a little distance you survey
The vineyards smiling 'neath the solar ray,
All seems one garden, strew'd with verdure o'er,
And Providence seems lavishly to pour
It's choicest gifts, exhausting all His store :

But, on approach, if you minutely scan
What seems effected by the pains of man;
Quickly you find it has been Fancy's task
To place before your eyes Deception's mask ;
For, sad reverse! on traversing the shore,
What beauteous seem'd is beauteous now no more.
But those defects, which on a nearer view
Efface the joy the bosom lately knew,
Reach not the eye, when from the vessel's side
You glance enraptur'd o'er the prospect wide ;
Here you perceive what well rewards the sight,
Exalts the soul and gives it to delight : .
The various objects strike the searching eye,
And almost swell the heart to ecstasy;
Successive beauties 'fore the senses fly,
And still you wonder at the fair variety.

The pyramidal mount, with pointed brow,
Threats seeming ruin to the town below;
And one might deem 'twas hither forceful hurl'd,
By the commotions of an earlier world.
Direct the gaze upon those glens beneath —
They seem the empires of uncourtly Death :
Delve after delve invite th' inquiring view,
Their drear and trackless windings to pursue —

Where stately Grandeur rears his throne sublime,
And seems t' have fix'd his seat to farthest time—
Tend too to slack Imagination's rein,
And to the mind impart her sterling gain.

A

BLANK SONNET,

ON

𝕾𝖔𝖑𝖎𝖙𝖚𝖉𝖊.

———

SWEET Solitude! With thee the tinctur'd mind
Regenerates and purifies anew!
Cleans'd by thy chast'ning hand, the morbid taints
Of lolling Luxury evaporate,
And leave sublim'd the soul. Thy verdant path
Invites the footstep where Content abides,
To lull the moanings of Disquietude,
And sooth the troubled bosom into rest.
As pois'nous vapours flee the noontide beam,
So the corruptions of a tamper'd heart
Disperse before serene Reflection's rays,
Bred 'neath the shielding wings of Solitude.
She proffers to her child the salve of Peace,
Cleanses the heart, and points the eye to Heav'n.

S O N G.

ONE morn as JULIA stroll'd along
  The hawthorn circled lawn,
And listen'd to the linnet's song,
  That caroll'd to the dawn;
A primrose in her path she spied,
  And pluck'd it from the stem;
Straight to her lips the flow'r applied,
  To sip it's dewy gem.

A bee that lay within it's bell *,
  Conceal'd from JULIA's eye,
Quitting, disturb'd, the fragrant cell,
  Spread out it's wings to fly;
But fast'ning first on JULIA's lip,
  Before it soar'd awing,
The honey'd sweets awhile did sip,
  Then flying, left it's sting.

* The reader must be here kind enough to fancy an *opening* primrose.

Here take a friendly hint, ye fair!
    Be cautious where ye kiss!
Of soft appearances beware,
    Lest ye be serv'd like this!
For man oft-times, of aspect meet,
    May lead your hearts amiss;
And then, too late, ye find deceit,
    Where ye had look'd for bliss.

A VISION.

In contemplating Nature's plan,
The crafts of woman and of man;
Their tendency to such pursuits,
As oft degrade them 'neath the brutes;
'Tis clear their reprobate intents
Arise from vicious precedents.
Did Vice her standard seldom rear,
Evil as rarely would appear,
The heart is never form'd impure —
Nor, until Vice extends her lure,
Does it, as infancy confesses,
Submit to Evil's foul caresses.
Had Virtue more unbounded sway,
The foe would fly her chaster ray;
But *that* on *precept* solely lives,
This palpable *example* gives;
One we but *hear*, the other *see*,
Grand source of worldly misery!

Vice ever holds resistless sway;
Whilst Virtue, baffled, stalks away.
What marvel is't that *striplings* fall,
When Vice has spread her snares for all?
Many who deprecate her charms,
Rush on and clasp her in their arms;
Whilst some who Virtue's garb affect,
Oft treat her precepts with neglect:
Where her instructions nought succeed,
Vice never fails to supersede—
Premises cease, the vision read.

Sleep's Regent o'er my plastic brain
Held undisturb'd and potent reign;
His dexter hand upheld a vase—
Somnific poppies fill'd it's space:
The DREAMS stood by him, which bestow
Their visions on the world below:
One gave a light and active bound,
And quickly lit on nether ground;
Young FANCY from his side had fled,
And clos'd her pinions o'er my head;
There taking rest, my sight she clear'd,
And here shall follow what appear'd.

Methought I wander'd o'er a plain —
Tho' lovely, small was the domain;
But strew'd with flow'rs of choicest hues,
Which love to sip the matin dews.
The lily, snow-drop, and the rose,
Their various beauties here disclose;
The violet, the daisy pied,
The primrose, Spring's prolific bride;
The hare-bell, jasmine full in blow,
In just, tho' varied order grow;
Symbolical of INNOCENCE,
Who here possess'd inheritance.
At first she deign'd to be my guide,
Till I had reach'd the farther side;
But left me then, because I plann'd
To trespass o'er the neighb'ring land.

Quitted by her I took my way,
Unheeding whither I might stray;
And travers'd many a pleasing spot,
Too beautiful to be forgot;
But came at length, I knew not where,
Till told it was the realm of CARE.
I merely then the borders prest,
Nor thought the churl would dare molest;

When, by the trespass, no intent
To vex or give offence was meant.
Methought he was a man austere,
Of aspect rugged and severe;
His limbs were clad in mean attire,
And oft his eye-balls roll'd in fire:
His jaws with pointed fangs were arm'd—
Devouring vermin o'er him swarm'd;
His matted locks were jetty black,
And monstrous loads oppress'd his back:
His cheeks were channell'd, and the tear
Of agony would oft appear;
Yet stern his brow, his eyes were wild—
He seem'd some foul abortive child.

After I'd hurried to and fro,
Quite undecided where to go,
And lacerated by the thorn
Which this drear region did adorn—
For briars in abundance grew,
With nettles, thorns, and thistles too—
Not distant far a vale I spy'd,
Where Art alone could be descry'd:
Here Nature had of old been rude,
And form'd a grove for Solitude;

Till Luxury the dame expell'd,
When all the sylvan tribe rebell'd:
And, whilst Confusion spoil'd the plain,
Her daughter Vice commenc'd her reign.
On all sides were delightful bow'rs,
Garnish'd with aromatic flow'rs;
And mirrors, to reflect the face,
Were seen in each convenient place;
By blind Profusion's hand were borne
The various freights from Plenty's horn;
Young crystal rills meander'd by,
And rippled on melodiously;
Art, too, refreshing gales produc'd,
Which ev'ry finer sense seduc'd:
All that might charm the carnal eye
Was furnish'd in variety;
Whate'er might cause the passions rise,
In ev'ry arbour struck the eyes;
Concupiscence, in lustful dress,
Hush'd in the lap of fond Excess;
Intemperance, with pimpled face,
Fast lock'd in Pleasure's lewd embrace: —
Much more I saw, but did not find
That *Prudence* had forsook my mind.

Consistent elegance portray'd,
Was all this simple path display'd.
The other which oppos'd mine eye,
Expos'd a vast variety;
The pink, the polyanthus gay,
And tulips in superb array,
With ev'ry gaudy colour'd flow'r
That decks mad Folly's varied bow'r,
Were seen abundant: tho' to view
Gigantic Grandeur's pageant grew,
As oft my gaze I cast around,
In no one spot could *Taste* be found;
And those gay flow'rs which struck the eye
Displeas'd the nerves olfactory.

The former's guide was neatly drest
In clean tho' very homely vest;
A crystal on her breast she wore,
Her hand a sprig of laurel bore;
A radiance beam'd around her brow,
As fair and pure as falling snow;
Her features bore expression mild,
And, tho' she very rarely smil'd,
Strong and persuasive was her speech,
Yet such as any mind might reach:

Her words impressive, but refin'd,
For Wisdom's torch illum'd her mind.
Long I survey'd the vestal dame,
And ask'd her to declare her name ;
She told me VIRTUE, and employ'd
By Happiness to be the guide
Of all her worthy votaries,
Who wish'd — life o'er — to seek the skies.
Straight to the other path I went,
And sought it's gaudy President :
Her dress was all a tinsel glare,
'Neath jewels groan'd her braided hair ;
Her bosom heaving to the sight,
Bred wishes of impure delight ;
A cestus bound her slender waist,
Her loins a muslin vesture grac'd,
So flimsy, that it half reveal'd
Beauties but partially conceal'd.
The dang'rous nymph was form'd to please,
But in her bosom lurk'd Disease.
Her limbs were exquisite of grace,
But Lust was couchant in her face.
I found her name was PLEASURE. She
Was hir'd by ragged Misery,
To lure all those whom Vice misled,
By smirking Folly's dang'rous aid,

And bring them to her dreary cell,
Where all the broods of Torment dwell;
Where, as a sentinel, Despair
Watches with unrelaxing care;
Where all is drear unsocial gloom,
And Happiness can never bloom.

First Virtue beckon'd my advance—
My sense was deep in Folly's trance—
Whilst Pleasure press'd me in her arms,
And fed mine eyes with siren charms.
By fell Delusion stricken blind,
I left bland Virtue's path behind,
And should have enter'd Pleasure's reign,
Where breed the foulest imps of Pain,
Had not an angel shape appear'd,
And bade me stop.—The voice was heard;
And when the graceful form I view'd,
'Twas GUARDIAN FRIENDSHIP 'fore me stood;
I felt abash'd — yet scarce knew why —
As if some angry judge were nigh.
He took a cup; in mute surprise
I felt him wash my blinded eyes;
Quick was the clouded vision clear'd,
And baleful Pleasure disappear'd.

VOL. I.   P

The liquid which the vessel fil'd,
From *Flow'rs* of *Reason* was distill'd :
Soon as was wash'd the misty ken,
The optic felt it's pow'r again.
Enabled now t' explore my heart,
I pluck'd from thence the poison'd dart :
Soon was my panting breast compos'd,
For the late wound that instant clos'd.
Empower'd now that path to scan
Into the which I nearly ran,
I saw — but from the entrance far —
The human passions waging war ;
Calamities in swarms I view'd,
And in the middle Pleasure stood.
There Want, Disease, and Poverty,
Wo, Waspishness, and Cruelty,
Distress, Vexation, Peevishness,
Pain, Mis'ry, Grief, and Wretchedness,
Were striving all, in furious mood :—
Each suck'd it's prostrate victim's blood,
Fed on his vitals, tore his heart,
And mangled ev'ry tender part.
Disgusted at the scene, I turn'd,
And man's prevailing folly mourn'd ;
My conscious bosom hove a sigh,
And trembled at Mortality.

I now look'd down the adverse way,
Where Virtue held more gentle sway:
Here Innocence I first espied,
With the chaste Vestal by her side;
Humanity with Mercy twin'd,
And mild Good-nature lagg'd behind:
Justice, Benevolence, and Love,
With Peace and Concord seem'd to move;
United by the binding tie
Of fond endearing Amity.

Delighted, I resolv'd outright
To live in humbler Virtue's sight:
But, as the just resolve I made,
And, raptur'd, sought the peerless Maid,
Hale Morn had chas'd away the night,
And fled the vision from my sight.

END OF THE FIRST VOLUME.

J. MOYES, PRINTER,
Greville Street, Hatton Garden, London.

CPSIA information can be obtained
at www.ICGtesting.com
Printed in the USA
BVOW03*1447301117
501641BV00002B/7/P

This spot,—which look'd a Paradise,
But only such to partial eyes—
To lolling Luxury was giv'n
By Indolence, revil'd of Heav'n.
The former had a feast provided
For sporting Cupids, who presided;
With bows and arrows all equipt,
And ev'ry barb in poison dipt.
They shot at ev'ry one who past,
And I receiv'd a wound at last:
The little urchin twang'd his yew—
Against my breast an arrow flew;
The speedy wound did rankle sore,
For love was barter'd to a w——e.
Seeking at length the valley's bound,
With toil I gain'd the bord'ring ground:
Two paths appear'd, but different quite,
I paus'd to fix upon the right.
The hedges of the first I view'd,
With evergreens were thickly strew'd;
Their unimposing forms they rear'd,
But 'midst the leaves no flow'rs appear'd:
Yet now and then, amid the green,
The plant call'd sensitive was seen;
Which—type of her who govern'd here—
Shrinks from the touch in seeming fear:—